INSIGHT GUIDES

GREAT BREAKS

BELFAST

Walking Eye App

YOUR FREE EBOOK AVAILABLE THROUGH THE WALKING EYE APP

Your guide now includes a free eBook to your chosen destination, for the same great price as before. Simply download the Walking Eye App from the App Store or Google Play to access your free eBook.

HOW THE WALKING EYE APP WORKS

Through the Walking Eye App, you can purchase a range of eBooks and destination content. However, when you buy this book, you can download the corresponding eBook for free. Just see below in the grey panel where to find your free content and then scan the QR code at the bottom of this page.

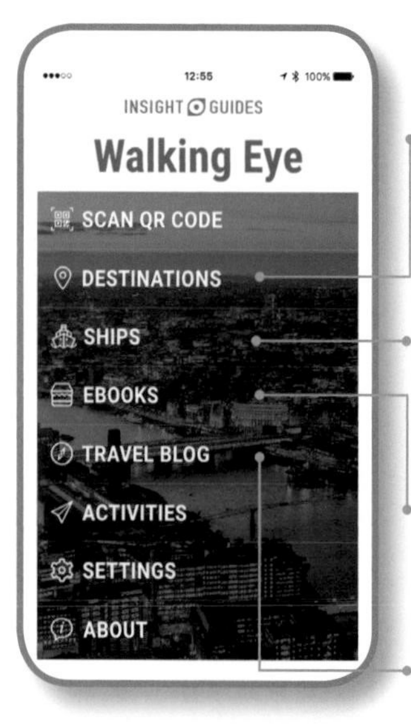

Destinations: Download essential destination content featuring recommended sights and attractions, restaurants, hotels and an A–Z of practical information, all available for purchase.

Ships: Interested in ship reviews? Find independent reviews of river and ocean ships in this section, all available for purchase.

eBooks: You can download your free accompanying digital version of this guide here. You will also find a whole range of other eBooks, all available for purchase.

Free access to travel-related blog articles about different destinations, updated on a daily basis.

HOW THE EBOOKS WORK

The eBooks are provided in EPUB file format. Please note that you will need an eBook reader installed on your device to open the file. Many devices come with this as standard, but you may still need to install one manually from Google Play.

The eBook content is identical to the content in the printed guide.

HOW TO DOWNLOAD THE WALKING EYE APP

1. Download the Walking Eye App from the App Store or Google Play.
2. Open the app and select the scanning function from the main menu.
3. Scan the QR code on this page – you will then be asked a security question to verify ownership of the book.
4. Once this has been verified, you will see your eBook in the purchased ebook section, where you will be able to download it.

Other destination apps and eBooks are available for purchase separately or are free with the purchase of the Insight Guide book.

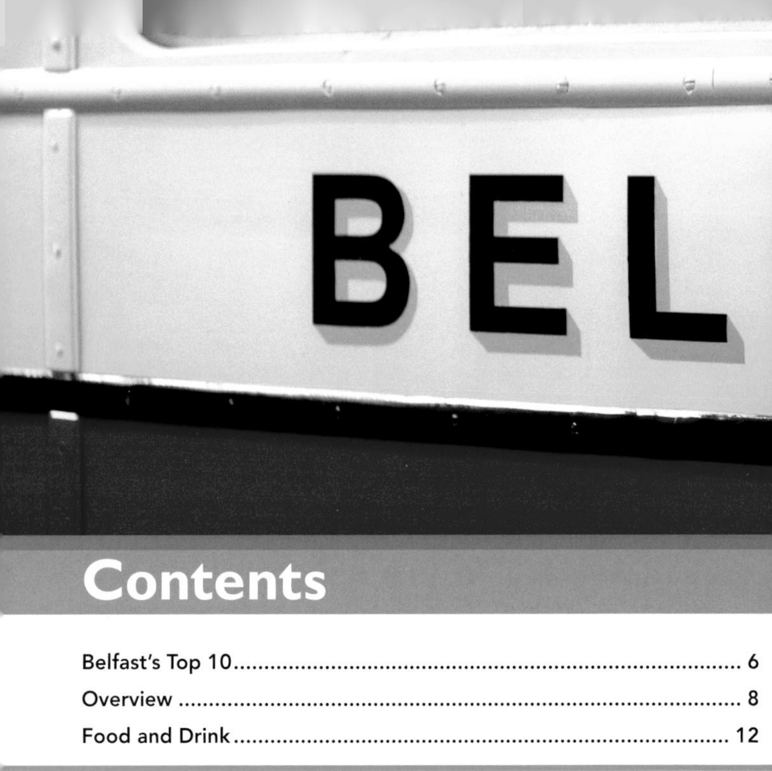

Contents

Travel Tips

Belfast's Top 10

From imposing architecture, a Victorian legacy and a proud industrial heritage, to a diverse, spectacular landscape, here at a glance are just a few of the attractions Belfast and Northern Ireland have to offer.

▲ **Botanic Gardens.** Popular since Victorian times, this colourful park features a classic 1839 Palm House. See page 53.

▲ **Crown Liquor Saloon.** A Victorian bar that is so ornate the National Trust bought it. See page 22.

▲ **Causeway Coastal Route.** A spectacular route along Antrim's coast taking in such alluring fishing villages as Cushenden. See page 90.

▶ **Giant's Causeway.** One of the wonders of the world, an astonishing array of basalt columns formed by the cooling of molten lava. See page 92.

◀ **City Hall.** This shameless imitation of St Paul's Cathedral dominates the city centre. See page 28.

▲ **Titanic heritage.** The doomed liner was built here and Titanic Belfast commemorates the legacy. See page 84.

▲ **Grand Opera House.** This oriental fantasy hosts all manner of events, from West End musicals to Shakespeare. See page 24.

▲ **Derry.** Europe's last walled city, besieged in 1689 and now the centre of an exhilarating social and cultural scene. See page 94.

▲ **Ulster Folk and Transport Museum.** Step back in time for a living history experience. See page 109.

▶ **Parliament Buildings.** Stormont is the setting for Northern Ireland's devolved government. See page 87.

Queen's Bridge over the Lagan.

Overview

A vibrant city

Belfast and Northern Ireland have emerged triumphant from the Troubles, rebuilding communities and promoting their urban vitality and spectacular landscapes.

Without its baggage of troubles, and the resultant 30 years of media coverage that sent its flames around the globe, Belfast could have been seen in another light: as an extravagance of pubs and churches; as a seaport rich in Victorian buildings, where the ill-fated *Titanic was built*; as a hub for the manufacture of Irish linen; as host to a fine university; as home to the late George Best, a footballing legend.

But Belfast was abandoned to a different fate and a troubled period of history. There was scant mention of the abundant *craic*, of the in-your-face northern humour, of pubs pulsing with music and of Guinness downed in the Crown Liquor Saloon.

Since the mid-1990s, Belfast has realised its pre-Troubles potential. That *craic* is now enjoyed in hip bars and hotels as well as traditional pubs. You can dance the night away at cutting-edge clubs and eat remarkably well before setting off on excursions to some of the finest scenery in the British Isles. A

century after its golden age, Belfast is finally coming into its own.

POSITION AND LANDSCAPE

Belfast sits in a saucer of hills in the northeast of Ireland, at the head of a broad sea lough at the mouth of the River Lagan, which flows into the Irish Sea. It is the capital of the six counties of Northern Ireland (Antrim, Armagh, Londonderry, Down, Fermanagh and Tyrone), founded in 1921.

Northern Ireland occupies just 17 percent of the island's landmass, but contains a high proportion of its physical attractions. The Antrim Coast Road is a marvel of engineering. Behind it lie the nine Glens of Antrim, a world of rugged scenery and weather-beaten farmers. On the northern coast, past long stretches of sandy beaches, lies the Giant's Causeway, a remarkable geological curiosity. County Fermanagh's lakelands and Lough Neagh, the largest sheet of inland water in the British Isles, are a draw for anglers and boating enthusiasts. Spectacular mountain ranges, the Sperrins and the Mournes, complete the picture.

THE ULSTER CHARACTER

Instead of the soft, beguiling brogue the world regards as distinctively Irish,

Parking space outside Queen's University.

A night out at the Duke of York pub.

the Northern Irish accent is harder, less melodious. Think Van Morrison rather than Enya. Some say it is an accent that adapts particularly well to rabble-rousing oratory, as exemplified by the province's best-known former politician, the late Reverend Ian Paisley.

Nor does the people's character conform to the Hollywood image of Irishness. Northern Protestants are generally regarded as being more earnest and less imaginative than northern Catholics, who are in turn judged to be less outgoing and less impulsive than their southern counterparts.

Stubbornness and a reluctance to compromise are more often seen as virtues than vices. Nevertheless, visitors are constantly surprised to encounter a warm welcome in Northern Ireland – as long, of course, as talk doesn't turn to politics.

TURBULENCE TO PEACE

As a result of the Anglo-Irish War of 1919–21, six of the nine counties of the province of Ulster became known as Northern Ireland, remaining part of the United Kingdom (with self-governance). The British government, glad to be rid of the troublesome Irish Question, ignored the problems in their forgotten province. But by the 1960s civil unrest was prevalent with students swelling the ranks of the Civil Rights Movement, marching to demand an end to discrimination in social housing and employment for Catholics. As old animosities flared up, Protestants began setting fire to Catholics' houses in Belfast. A moribund IRA resurrected itself to defend them. Protestant terrorist groups were formed in retaliation.

It took 30 years, the abolition of self-governance, the imposition of direct rule from Westminster, the creation of a Dublin–London political axis, major population shifts and the loss of more than 3,200 lives before the province voted in 1998 for peace through a power-sharing Assembly. But mutual suspicions remained and political deadlock forced the British government to suspend the Assembly until trust was established. It was touch-and-go, but five years of direct rule ended on 8 May 2007 when Ian Paisley and Sinn Féin's Martin McGuinness, who had never

Police charge a crowd of rioting demonstrators in 1870.

Go green and explore

The Northern Ireland Environment Agency is responsible for the management of a vast number of natural habitats, wildlife reserves and geological features throughout the country. Walking and cycling paths, both long distance and shorter city routes, are important features of a government-backed programme to encourage local people and visitors alike to get out of their cars. Ecotourism is the latest trend (www.greentraveller.co.uk; www.walkni.com; www.mournelive.com). The message from the tourist board is clear: go green and explore this beautiful land!

spoken before, sat down together as Northern Ireland's new leaders.

But with the late Martin McGuinness' resignation in January 2017 prompting a tight Assembly election, a fresh political deadlock emerged, throwing the future of Stormont's power-sharing government into question. Northern Ireland's political future is further complicated by the UK voting to leave the European Union in 2016, with the prospect of a hard border looming. The two main parties in Northern Ireland are currently both headed by women, the Democratic Unionist Party (DUP) by Arlene Foster and Sinn Féin by Michelle O'Neill.

Guide to Coloured Boxes

Eating
Fact
Green
Kids
Shopping
View

This guide is dotted with coloured boxes providing additional practical and cultural information to make the most of your visit. Here is a guide to the coding system.

Taking it easy in the Botanic Gardens.

A NEW BELFAST

Neither planners nor bombers were kind to Belfast. In the 1960s a lacklustre provincial civil service failed to recognise the vernacular environment that architect Charles Lanyon had created a century before. Great buildings were demolished, replaced by flaking concrete. The bombers had a go at much that was left, leaving a city rich in unplanned parking lots, with a few fine buildings standing out. The decline of the shipbuilding industry left the banks of the Lagan lying idle and looking derelict.

At the first signs of peace, fly-overs swept through inner-city villages, and Belfast rekindled its affection for its potent Victorian and Edwardian heritage. Laganside Corporation was a public body formed in 1989 to regenerate the Laganside. It captured a public imagination fired by Victor Robinson's keynote Waterfront Hall, and drew up plans for the Cathedral cultural quarter, now a centre of culture and trendy nightlife.

From City Hall south to the university, streets became packed with bars and nightclubs, attracting partygoers from Britain and further afield. Growth has continued with the development of the docks area and the opening of both the Metropolitan Arts Centre (MAC) and the boat-shaped Titanic Belfast, boosting tourism in the area.

Food and Drink

It wasn't until the peace process kicked in that good food became consistently easy to find in Belfast and throughout the province. Brilliant local food and imaginative chefs have transformed the eating out experience to make Belfast a 'foodie' city par excellence. Eating trends are changing rapidly with more choice and good, well-priced food available throughout the city. Having said that, the choice for vegetarians is still restricted, although demand for organic food is a selling point in an increasing number of restaurants. Throughout Northern Ireland eating establishments vary from seafront restaurants along the Causeway Coastal route to seafood bars at the foot of the Mourne Mountains, and from contemporary city restaurants in Belfast to hearty pub grub in beautiful rural spots.

Guinness tastes better in Belfast.

IRISH COOKING

A distinctive style of Irish cooking has started to emerge over the past years. A new generation of chefs takes pride in using indigenous foods, supported by the growing number of artisan food producers, to produce a lighter, modern style with an innovative spin on traditional Irish cooking.

Organic produce on display at a farmers' market.

But traditional food will always have a place in the hearts of the people of Northern Ireland, and most traditional dishes have their roots in potatoes and bread. No visit to Northern Ireland would be complete without experiencing an Ulster Fry, distinguished by its griddle breads – soda bread and potato farls – fried until crisp and golden. Bacon, sausages, an egg, a tomato and maybe some mushrooms complete the picture – and, of course, a pot of tea.

OTHER LOCAL SPECIALITIES

Champ: mashed potatoes with lots of butter, warm milk and chopped scallions (spring onions or shallots).
Dulse: a salty, seaweed snack, harvested by fishermen to supplement their income when fishing was slack.
Potato bread farl: a dense, earthy flat bread, made with potatoes, flour and buttermilk, cooked on a griddle.

Soda bread farl: thick, chunky soft bread, first baked in 19th-century Ireland when local peasants added baking soda to help the dough rise.
Wheaten bread: a brown bread made with whole-wheat flour.
Yellow man: crunchy golden confectionery that resembles honeycomb.
Boxty: starchy potato cake made with a 50:50 mix of cooked mashed potatoes and grated, strained, raw potato.

LOCAL PRODUCE

A mild climate and green and fertile land conjures up perfect agricultural country. Specialist farmers and artisan producers are plentiful in Northern Ireland and the region is rapidly gaining a reputation for its superb local producers: Lough Neagh is Europe's greatest source of eels; Finnebrogue venison has put Northern Ireland on the map in top restaurants; the much sought-after Comber potato is grown in the arable farmland of County Down; Kettyles of Fermanagh produces extra-mature, dry-aged beef from its grass-fed native herd; and Moyallon Foods is the first choice among local chefs when it comes to dry-cure bacon, sausages and prime beefburgers.

A lively atmosphere at St George's Market.

Bushmills Whiskey

Bushmills Irish Whiskey is the original and best-known whiskey to come out of the Old Bushmills Distillery in County Antrim. This smooth, rich blend of single malt and single grain has been produced for four centuries, since King James 1 granted a licence to distil in 1608. The whiskey is processed the same way today as it was 400 years ago – aged a minimum of five years in oak casks specially selected to bring out the golden hue using only 100 per cent barley.

FOOD SHOPPING

Soak up the atmosphere at Ireland's oldest covered market, St George's in Belfast, which is abundant with terrific fresh fish and seafood, meats from grass-reared stock and creamy Irish cheeses. Farmers' markets are great if you are on a self-catering holiday, planning a picnic, or just wanting to try authentic Irish foods and talk to artisan producers. The pick of the bunch are the Tyrone Farmers' Market in Dungannon and Omagh (tel: 028-8776 7259), the Comber Farmers' Market in County Down (www.combermarket.co.uk), the Walled City Artisan Market in Derry (tel: 028-7136 5151) and the Causeway Speciality Market in Coleraine (tel: 028-7034 7044).

Eating Out Price Guide

Two-course meal for one person, including a glass of wine.
£££ = over £25
££ = £15–25
£ = under £15

Late-night shopping in Donegall Square.

Tour 1

Around the City Centre

This 2-mile (4km) walk, in half a day, takes you to some of Belfast's prime attractions and venerable institutions, the perfect introduction to this vibrant city.

The city centre of Belfast saw its fair share of turbulence during the Troubles but has emerged as an attractive area with a mix of grandiose architectural gems, modern shops and stylish restaurants catering for a busy, cosmopolitan capital city.

Highlights

- Linen Hall Library
- Scottish Provident Institution
- Ulster Hall
- Crown Liquor Saloon
- Grand Opera House
- Royal Belfast Academical Institution

WELCOME CENTRE

An excellent starting point is the **Visit Belfast Welcome Centre** ❶ (9 Donegall Square North; tel: 028-9024 6609; http://visitbelfast.com; June–Sept Mon–Sat 9am–7pm, Oct–May until 5.30pm, Sun 11am–4pm all year) where you can pick up informative brochures and get advice on accommodation, attractions, tours and transport from the multilingual staff. The centre also stocks a range of maps and general information on Northern Ireland; a separate desk is run by Failte Ireland which supplies details on places to visit in the Irish Republic. If you're unable to check into your hotel until later, you may leave your luggage here while you explore the city.

Researching Narnia

Linen Hall Library has added a collection of books by or about C.S. Lewis (1898–1963, see also Tour 9), the Belfast-born-and-raised Christian writer and author of the *Narnia Chronicles*. Visitors can access all the collections, although only members can borrow books. Public workshops are occasionally held, including drama workshops exploring *The Lion, the Witch and the Wardrobe* and the land of Narnia, for children aged 8 and above.

LINEN HALL LIBRARY

Just a few doors along, at 17 Donegall Square North, the **Linen Hall Library** ❷ (tel: 028-9032 1707; www.linenhall.com; Mon–Fri 9.30am–5.30pm, Sat until 4pm) is the last public subscription library left in Ireland. It has played a vigorous part in Belfast's cultural life for two centuries. Thomas Russell, a founding member, was arrested at its earlier premises in Ann Street for his part in the United Irishmen uprising of 1798.

The library's present location is a three-storey, five-bay building with stucco mouldings on its windows. The most eminent of the architects of Victorian Belfast, Charles Lanyon, designed the building as a linen warehouse of greyish-yellowish brick with a dressing of Victorian detail on its Georgian proportions. Inside, an impressive brass-railed stone staircase leads to the muted calm of reading rooms redolent with the aromas of the book stacks, its walls lined with heavy wooden glass-fronted bookcases and stained-glass windows commemorating famous writers.

Sensitively restored at no little cost, it now has a modern café and a well-stocked shop of literary souvenirs. The library is still a venue for regular cultural activities, including literary lectures, drama, poetry recitations and exhibitions, but its main attraction remains its unique collections. Chief among them is a major Irish and Local Studies collection, but many visitors come for its unrivalled Northern Ireland political collection from the Troubles, now running to some quarter of a million items. For those interested in cartographic prison history, a map of H-Block 7 used in the IRA Maze escape in 1983, is displayed in a cabinet in the political research room.

DONEGALL SQUARE WEST

Just opposite, facing the west side of City Hall, you can trace the industrial heritage of Belfast from carvings high up on the pale Giffnock sandstone of the vast **Scottish Provident Institution** ❸ on Donegall Square West. The building has almost as much Ed-

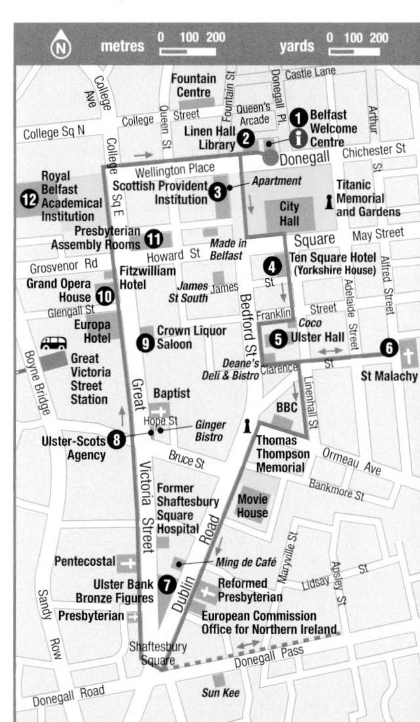

The book-lined walls of the Linen Hall Library.

wardian pomp and presence as the City Hall. Cherubs work at their ABCs on a Gutenberg printing press, and easily identified are an anchor and hammer for shipbuilding, plus skeins of linen yarn and a spinning wheel, the tools of ropemaking.

Below, less finely carved heads, copied from Thomas Fitzpatrick's work on what is now the Malmaison hotel (see page 125) in Victoria Street, represent the people to whom a commercially buoyant city exported its goods: an Englishman, benign and plump; an Asian tribal chief with his nose-ring; an African; and an indigenous native American with high cheekbones.

An area once home to many of the world's great linen manufacturers.

Modern Belfast

In stark contrast to its venerable host, within which it has prospered for some years, Apartment (see page 27) has become a rather overused symbol of the new, chic Belfast. A stylish bar and restaurant with an all-day menu, music at night, and clear views of City Hall, its arrival in a city centre that had been almost redundant in terms of entertainment during the Troubles signalled a new kind of venue for a younger generation more interested in cappuccinos and cocktails than political arguments or sectarian division. Such has been the avalanche of cool clubs, bars and cafés ever since, it now seems almost reassuringly traditional.

Linen district

Walk east along Donegall Square South to the former **Yorkshire House**, on the corner of Donegall Square South and Linenhall Street, which was built in 1862 as a three-storey, 18-bay linen warehouse and features a series of Heroes' Heads between first-floor windows, including George Washington, Isaac Newton, Homer and Michelangelo. The building has been transformed into the luxurious **Ten Square hotel ❹** (see page 125) with a popular bar and restaurant.

Turn right here to view Linen Hall House at 13–19 Linenhall Street. Built in 1855, the building spent much of its life serving the linen trade, as did No. 40, and to the right in Franklin Street, Nos 25–27.

At the end of Franklin Street turn south, where it is easy to spot the one-time linen warehouses on Bedford Street, particularly the warm brown sandstone mass of Ewart House (No. 17), built as an Italian Renaissance palace for a linen dynasty.

Ulster Hall

Further along Bedford Street you will see the Italianate stucco of W.J. Barre's **Ulster Hall ❺** (tel: 028-9033 4400; www.ulsterhall.co.uk). Completed in 1862 as a ballroom, it became the largest music hall in the British Isles, its airy spaciousness and excellent acoustics also providing a resounding platform for the rallies of the Irish nationalist politicians Charles Stewart Parnell and Patrick Pearse, and for David Lloyd George, British prime minister from 1916 to 1922.

The hall was reopened in 2009 following an extensive two-year refurbishment, which saw new seating and lighting facilities, an exhibition on its history, and much more. Decorated in the colour scheme Barre wanted but couldn't afford, it is now the home of the Ulster Orchestra and features again the famous paintings of Belfast history by Joseph Carey.

Along from the Ulster Hall, the New York-style **Deane's Deli** (see page 27) and Parisian-flavoured Vin Cafe (the Deli Store during the day) are under the auspices of Belfast's renowned chef, Michael Deane.

St Malachy's Church

Turning left into Clarence Street, at the far end stands the dusky red-brick exterior of the Roman Catholic **St Malachy's Church ❻** framed in the east. Designed by Thomas Jackson in 1880, this romantic church is a splendid turreted and castellated excursion into Tudor Gothic, its panelled door studded and topped with armorial

Star performers

The Ulster Hall stages all kinds of concerts, from regular Ulster Orchestra gigs to rock and pop stars, kickboxing tournaments, beer festivals and much else. Rock fans will know that the Rolling Stones played the Hall in 1964 and that Led Zeppelin's *Stairway to Heaven* had its stage debut here in 1971. The hall's massive Mulholland organ attracts a different fan base.

Ulster Hall has played host to many famous figures.

The intricate fan-vaulted ceiling and striking stained-glass windows of St Malachy's Church.

shields. However, it is the church's interior that makes the visitor gasp.

The dazzling fan-vaulted ceiling, a confection of creamy and frothy plasterwork, has been likened to a wedding cake turned inside out. In fact, it is an echo of Henry VII's Chapel in Westminster Abbey. Many of the original unpolished Irish oak fittings have disappeared but the organ is a century and a half old.

The church's chief benefactor, Captain Thomas Griffiths, understood that it would become the city's Roman Catholic cathedral, which accounts for the extravagance of decoration. The Great Bell installed in 1868 was once wrapped in felt to quieten its toll, for its resonance was claimed to interfere with distillation processes in Dunville's Whiskey Distillery, which stood nearby. The church reopened after an extensive restoration in 2009. Along the southeast wall gazing out in contemplative mood with his brown eyes and torn chocolate brown coat, is the newly cleaned statue of the Ragged Saint, St Benedict Joseph Labre.

Return west up Clarence Street, and catch a glimpse of the Black Mountain in the distance, before taking the second left south along Linenhall Street to emerge on Ormeau Avenue, where the city's reservoir once shimmered.

ORMEAU AVENUE

The **BBC Broadcasting House** (tel: 028-9033 8000; tours Mon, Tue and Wed noon; free), opened in 1941, is on the right of the avenue and is one of the finest Art Deco buildings in the city. Turn right out of Linenhall Street. Almost unnoticed at the junction of Ormeau Avenue and Bedford Street, shaded under dusty trees, stands the **Thomas Thompson Memorial**, erected in memory of the founder of the city's Home for the Incurable. It takes the form of an elaborate crusty red Aberdeen granite and sandstone drinking fountain bearing the legend 'Who so drinketh of the water that I shall give him... shall never thirst again'. Thompson, a naval surgeon during the Napoleonic Wars, served in Latin America and the West Indies, gaining knowledge that enabled him to combat outbreaks of cholera, smallpox, dysentery and typhus in Belfast, not least during the Great Famine of the 1840s when the potato crop failed. Among the medieval-style heads carved below the spire of Thompson's fountain is one of the good doctor himself, sporting luxuriant whiskers and a monocle.

DUBLIN ROAD

Follow the **Dublin Road**, which runs south towards Shaftesbury Square. This is a fairly concentrated stretch of (largely Asian) restaurants, pubs, fast-food joints and fashion shops, beginning with one of Belfast's largest cinema complexes, the multi-screen Movie House at No. 14 (tel: 033-001 5151) – although the cinema's future is under threat with plans afoot to redevelop the area.

When the restaurants started burgeoning in the 1990s, locals referred to the stretch as the Golden Mile, but the gold glistens less than it once seemed to. For authentic Chinese

Speak like a local

The Ulster-Scots Agency (tel: 028-9023 1113; www.ulsterscotsagency.com; Mon–Fri 10am–4pm, free) was set up after the Good Friday peace agreement of 1998. Its remit is to promote the Ulster-Scots language – some see it as a dialect rather than a language – but whatever the interpretation, it permeates local culture in the form of road signs and advertisements. The centre has a large selection of free literature on Ulster-Scots literature and history, and the staff will supply you with ideas for day trips from the city to explore the culture. Look out for the welcome sign on the door encouraging visitors to 'Gie the door a chap' which translates as 'Please knock the door'. When former US President, Barack Obama, visited Belfast in June 2013 for the G8 summit in Northern Ireland, he was greeted at the international airport by a Stormont government minister with the words: 'Fair fae ye', meaning 'Welcome.'

Go behind the scenes on a tour of the BBC's Broadcasting House.

Dining out in Shaftesbury Square.

food check out **The Chilli House** at No 85 (028-9031 3666). The Sichuan menu features traditional favourites such as hotpot, *shui zhu* pork and ginger sea bass.

Looking a little out of place, further down the road, is the impressive Shaftesbury Square **Reformed Presbyterian Church**, which dates from 1890. Next door to the church is a modern office block housing the European Commission in Northern Ireland (028-9024 0708; www.ec.europa.eu/northernireland), including an information point open to the public.

A detour left from Shaftesbury Square, named after the 7th Earl of Shaftesbury, leads to a curious but rewarding blend of antiquity and motorbike salesrooms in Donegall Pass; the streets off it are named after trees in the wood it once passed through. Here amid walls of loyalist graffiti are several excellent antiques and fine arts shops and some of Belfast's more interesting Chinese restaurants: the **Same Happy**, at 40 Donegall Pass, and the atmospheric – and, for Belfast, unusually authentic – **Sun Kee** at Nos 43–7 Donegall Passage.

Donegall Pass is a loyalist section between two republican areas.

Shaftesbury Square

Return to **Shaftesbury Square**, which itself is not particularly prepossessing but it does contain the popular Italian restaurant **Speranza** behind a huge glass frontage.

High up on the **Ulster Bank**'s Portland stone at the corner of Dublin Road and Great Victoria Street is one of the best public art pieces in Northern Ireland. This pair of floating **bronze figures** ❼ by the sculptor Elisabeth Frink has been dubbed 'Draft and Overdraft' by local people, who, with typical Belfast humour, already called this end wall of the former Ulster Bank, Clark's Gable, after the bank's then director.

Sculpture of flying figures on the side of Ulster Bank.

GREAT VICTORIA STREET

Proceeding north, the route follows **Great Victoria Street**, once an avenue of fine red-brick and stucco terraced houses. But the bombers of the 1970s continued what the planners had only in part achieved a decade earlier: the demotion of the street's southern half to a mix of car parks and brutalist 1960s constructions. Now little but the ice cream-coloured stucco styling of the 1860s **Presbyterian Church** and the upper storeys of Victorian Richmond Terrace, north of the Ulster Bank, remain to tell of its former dignity.

Further up the road is the entirely rebuilt **Apostolic Evangelical Pentecostal Church**, in a building that in the 1870s was the city's first synagogue. Vere Foster, the revolutionary educational philanthropist who helped many get to America in the famine years of the 1840s, lived and died at No. 115.

The polychrome brick building on the terrace's town side, **Shaftesbury Square Hospital**, designed by W.J. Barre in 1867, originally cared for those with ophthalmic problems and more recently for those suffering another kind of darkness: substance abuse. Water was a concern of the painter Paul Henry's father, minister at the Great Victoria Street **Bap-**

Eco-friendly hotel

The Fitzwilliam Hotel (see page 124) in Great Victoria Street is a seriously 'green' hotel. Opened in 2009, its credentials as an environmentally friendly establishment were built into the very fabric of the building, with specialist heating and ventilation systems to manage the energy used. Efficient management of the recycling of waste is another key issue. Guests are encouraged to contribute, by turning off electrical appliances and using the laundry service for towels responsibly.

The atmospheric interior of the Fitzwilliam Hotel.

tist Church on the corner of Hope Street. He scandalised his 1870 congregation by announcing he had lost faith in total-immersion baptism. The tiny house abutting it is claimed to be the city's narrowest. The street also houses **The Ginger Bistro**, a lively restaurant for lunch or dinner serving local artisan beers.

On the other side of the road on Hope Street, Days Hotel, a huge modern building that apes the functional 1960s architecture that disfigured much of this area, makes up in value what its exterior lacks in aesthetic appeal. Back on Great Victoria Street, to catch a flavour of the local dialect, call into the **Ulster-Scots Agency** ❽ at Nos 68–72, a government-funded organisation promoting the study of Ulster-Scots as a living language (see page 19).

Crown Liquor Saloon

Further on along Great Victoria Street is the Victorian Baroque **Crown Liquor Saloon** ❾ (tel: 028-9024 3187; www.crownbar.com), Belfast's most famous pub. Bought in 1978 by the National Trust (on the recommendation of Sir John Betjeman who referred to it as a 'many-coloured cavern'), it was once the Ulster Railway Hotel, dating from 1895, the same year as the Opera House, and was also restored by Robert McKinstry.

It is a cream, three-storey stucco building whose ground-floor bar is lavishly tiled in many colours and whose snugs – with bronze match strikers and a bell that wags a flag to summon service – are guarded by griffin and lions. The superb tiling, glasswork and ornamental woodwork are the creation of Italian craftsmen, brought to Belfast in the 1880s to work on Catholic churches. In 2007 decades of generic dirt and dust were removed and the bar emerged gleaming and glistening from a 21st-century restoration.

The ceiling is embossed, the oysters and Guinness admirable, the

The richly burnished red and gold ceiling and decorative mosaic floor of the Crown Liquor Saloon, a fine example of Victoriana.

A whistle-stop ride round the city by bus.

waiters amenable and the customers a mixed bunch of stage hands, actors, journalists, travel writers, students and open-mouthed tourists. Despite moving into the social-media age, it remains one of the most authentic Victorian bars you can find.

Bars, buses and hotels

That is not something that can be said for **Robinson's Bar** (38–40 Great Victoria Street; tel: 028-9024 7447; http://saloon.robinsonsbar.co.uk), two doors north, which was bombed in 1991, gutting the interior, but has been rebuilt, its exterior faithful to the original 1846 design. It is now home to five bars, including Fibber Magees, which hosts traditional Irish music sessions. It also has the strikingly designed BT1 bar (named after Belfast's most fashionable postcode) in the basement, plus the Bistro restaurant/bar upstairs and, in the loft area, a traditional sports bar, the Pool Loft Bar.

Across the road fronting the entrance to the Europa Bus Centre, pose Louise Walsh's two life-sized bronzes (1992), titled *Monument to the Unknown Worker*. Amelia Street was once the bordello area, but the sculptor rejected the original idea of depicting prostitutes, and instead made this in tribute to low-paid working women. Here, too is the **Europa Hotel** (see page 124), from the comforts of which three decades of reporters covered the Troubles. It is notorious for being Europe's 'most bombed hotel', being the victim of 33 IRA bombs during this tumultuous period. The Europa remains a part of Belfast nightlife.

Taxi tours

One of the best ways to see Belfast is by taxi. These can be picked up in the city centre and take in the major and some lesser-known sights with the expert guides imparting their first-hand knowledge. Most tours of the city last around 1 hour 30 minutes and you should come away knowing a great deal more about Belfast's troubled past and hopes for the future. Details from the Belfast Welcome Centre.

A tour round the murals.

The Grand Opera House.

Grand Opera House

The street's honeypot is another riot of Victorian Baroque, the **Grand Opera House** ⓾ (tel: 028-9024 1919; www.goh.co.uk), although now somewhat dwarfed by the Europa Hotel. Designed by Frank Matcham and located on the corner of Glengall Street, the theatre, which opened in 1895, is an oriental fantasy where even the ventilation lantern has a Moorish air to it. It hosts touring Shakespearean productions, opera, ballet, concerts and touring West End musicals.

High on its frontage, a naked bronze Mercury takes flight and Shakespeare looks on approvingly. But it is the interior that really delights, a riot of crimson and gold leaf with gilded elephant heads supporting the boxes and a heavenly ceiling mural. The theatre languished unloved as a cinema for much of the 1960s and was almost abandoned in the 1970s as a result of damage caused by a series of terrorist bombs.

Thanks to a £9-million refurbishment in 2006, extended wing space means the historic venue can now accommodate the biggest West End productions. There's also a bright, spacious foyer, restaurant and bars and an intimate performance space, the Baby Grand. If you can't make it to a show, then the next best thing is to join a one-hour behind the scenes tour. Check with the theatre for times of these as they can change.

Presbyterian Assembly Rooms

Diagonally opposite the Opera House, on the corner of Howard Street, is the rusticated sandstone Tudor Gothic bulk of the **Presbyterian Assembly Rooms** ⓫, the essential English-

Opera House greats

The oriental-style Grand Opera House has played host to many international stars over the years. Sarah Bernhardt, Orson Welles and Laurel and Hardy have all appeared here in their day. Italian tenor Luciano Pavarotti made his UK debut here in 1963 in Puccini's *Madame Butterfly*, and local boy Van Morrison's album *Live at the Grand Opera House* (reissued in 2008) was recorded here in 1984.

The Oriental-style architecture of the Grand Opera House.

The facade of the Royal Belfast Academical Institution (RBAI).

ness of its mullioned windows made dour by Scots corbelling and a crown spire copied from St Giles' Cathedral, Edinburgh. The doorway arch and oriel window above are carved with biblical burning bushes and 14 angels. The contest for its design in 1899 was clouded in unbiblical scandal, however – the winner being the church's architect who devised the competition. The exterior turret clock was the first in these islands to use electricity to drive its cogs and ring its 12-bell carillon of 28 tunes.

Today the ground floor is given over to an elegant shopping centre, the Spires Mall, with shops and a café. The majestically polygonal Assembly Room upstairs, still one of the most impressive venues in Belfast, can be hired for conferences and concerts.

Royal Belfast Academical Institution

North of Jury's Hotel opposite the Assembly Rooms, Great Victoria Street becomes College Square East. It takes its name from the fine square lawn that complemented the Georgian symmetry of the dusky red-brick **Royal Belfast Academical Institution ⓬**. Now laid back beyond lawns, its spare elegance owing much to designs by the great English architect Sir John Soane, it is the city's finest building. Belfast's first major centre of learning, the RBAI was set up to cater for all the major denominations of Christianity and remains one of Northern Ireland's best schools.

In 1902, debts forced the governors to sell off land. Amid controversy, the Municipal Technical Institute was built. The style is pompous Baroque Revivalist, its four copper-domed turrets are impressive, and the city's coat of arms is set above the main doorway. This is now known as Belfast Metropolitan College – which also boasts a striking new campus in the Titanic quarter.

But the loss of green sward, and the education of labourers, destroyed the vista of College Square East and North, and the square's cachet as the address for surgeons and academics. The tall houses soon fell, first to commerce, then to the bomb.

The 'Black Man' statue on his plinth is of Dr Cooke, a Presbyterian cleric who was strongly against political liberalism.

WELLINGTON PLACE

To return to the Linen Hall Library, cross the road and go via Wellington Place, passing the 'Black Man' on his plinth. This 1876 statue of 19th-century, rabble-rousing Presbyterian cleric, Dr Henry Cooke, who opposed political liberalism, is not actually black but green. It is made of copper, which has turned green after being oxidised by the elements.

The original figure, made of bronze, painted black and later moved to the City Hall, was of the 1885 Earl of Belfast. The reverend, whom Daniel O'Connell called 'Bully Cooke', has his back turned to the Academy whose notions on equality and religious tolerance he desperately opposed.

Only Nos 7–11 of the original 1830s houses in **Wellington Place** remain. Named after the Duke of Wellington, who spent much of his boyhood at Annadale in the south of the city, this is now a street of boutiques, cafés and gift shops (see box), which leads us back to our starting place.

Chic shopping

Wellington Street is one of the most popular shopping areas in the city. Seen as setting trends, it is frequented by the fashionable young Belfast shopper, who favours boutiques such as Envoy, selling designer clothes, footwear and accessories. Also check out Octopus's Garden for three floors of vinyl records and vintage clothing.

Designer labels on show.

Eating Out

Apartment
2 Donegall Square; tel: 028-9099 4120; www.apartmentbelfast.com; tea/coffee Mon–Sat from 7am, dining Mon–Sat noon–9pm, Sun 1–8pm.
With splendid views of City Hall and a sleek modern interior, Apartment has a good reputation and is an elegant choice at any time of day. ££

Clements Café
4 Donegall Square West; tel: 028-9024 9988; http://clementscoffee.com; Mon–Fri 7am–5pm, Sat 9am–5pm.
If you want some of the best Fairtrade coffee in town, head for Clements. It delivers great sandwiches, cakes, bagels and juices in a comfortable, stylish interior. There are ten branches dotted around Belfast. £

Coco
7–11 Linenhall Street; tel: 028-9031 1150; www.cocobelfast.com; lunch Sun–Fri noon–3pm, dinner Mon–Sat from 5.30pm.
Coco has rapidly gained a reputation as one of Belfast's best and coolest restaurants. The chef/co-owner Jason More pays great attention to the menu, with locally sourced ingredients taking pride of place. Try the blackened monkfish with wet polenta, cavolo nero, pancetta, pine nuts and sage. ££–£££

Deane's Deli and Bistro
42–4 Bedford Street; tel: 028-9024 8830; www.michaeldeane.co.uk; Mon–Fri 8am– 10pm; Sat 9am–10pm.
Popular with local office workers, this establishment is part of the Deane empire. The bistro serves classics with a modern twist – beer-battered haddock and chips and beefburgers in brioche buns, plus vegetarian options. If you want something a little lighter, you could head next door to the Vin Cafe. ££

The Fitzwilliam Hotel
1–3 Great Victoria Street; tel: 028-9044 2080; lunch, afternoon tea and dinner daily.
One of Belfast's newest and smartest hotel restaurants set amid chic surroundings. The food is modern, uncomplicated and full of flavour. £££

The Ginger Bistro
7–8 Hope Street; tel: 028-9024 4421; www.gingerbistro.com; lunch Thu–Sat noon–3pm, dinner Mon–Sat from 5.30pm.
Locally sourced seafood such as fillet of hake or sea bass comes highly recommended at this always-busy restaurant. The wines are first class, too, but for something different try the malt-flavoured handcrafted Belfast ales or lagers from the Mountains of Mourne. ££

James Street South
21 James Street South; tel: 028-9043 4310; www.jamesstreetsouth.co.uk; lunch Wed–Sat 12.30pm–2.30pm, dinner Mon–Sat from 5.30pm.
An exciting and innovative spot, with top-class cooking and service to match, with a classic European/ Mediterranean-style menu. Head Chef David Gillmore serves up dishes such as County Antrim beef fillet, violet mustard, broccoli and blue cheese. For a cheaper alternative, try the Bar and Grill next door – it's owned by the same company. ££–£££

Sun Kee
43–7 Donegall Pass; tel: 028-9031 2233; daily noon–11.30pm.
Located opposite the police station, this is one of Ireland's most authentic and well-regarded Chinese restaurants, and run by the Lo family. But do come prepared to be adventurous, not to rely on old favourites. ££

A statue of Queen Victoria stands in the grounds of City Hall.

Tour 2

City Hall to Donegall Place

Tracing the footsteps of major political figures and the city's industrial heritage, this walk (around 2.5 miles/4km and half a day) runs through the heart of everyday city life.

This route explores the area north of City Hall, a buzzing area where Belfast people go about their everyday lives. These streets are rich in stories of political figures such as Henry Joy McCracken, and have witnessed the prosperity of many industries, from linen production and newspaper publishing to boot making and distilling. There are architectural delights that utilise the city's typical red sandstone, and the legacies of W.J. Barre and Charles Lanyon. City Hall is at the centre of Belfast life, both geographically and politically, and is the most appropriate place to start. Many people gather here every day, just opposite the Tourist Information Office, before setting out to explore or beginning a day's work.

Highlights

- City Hall
- The entries
- First Presbyterian Church
- Queen's Arcade
- Former Robinson & Cleaver's

CITY HALL

This city of red-brick terraces and politico-historical folk is ruled from inside the marbled halls of Sir Brumwell Thomas's 1906 wedding-cake **City Hall** ❶ (Donegall Square; tel: 028-9032 0202; tours Mon–Fri 11am, 2pm, 3pm, Sat 2pm, 3pm; free). City Hall dominates the commercial heart of Belfast, imposing itself on the skyline from all angles, and is well worth investigating. Conceived in response to Queen Victoria's award of city status to Belfast in 1888, building began in 1898 on the site of the former White Linen Hall, and took eight years to complete (amid criticism of its escalating costs; the final figure of around £360,000 was nearly twice the original budget).

Once a symbol of unionist power, City Hall's Council Chamber saw an even split of nationalist and unionist councillors by its centenary year of 2006, thanks to Belfast's changing demographics. The hall reopened in October 2009 after a two-year restoration programme, which resulted in the Bobbin coffee shop (closed for refurbishment until spring 2017) and two permanent exhibitions focusing on Belfast industries from the 17th century to the present day. Since 2012, the Union Jack flag is, controversially, only allowed to be flown on 18 designated days a year.

Open-top bus tours

Hop on, hop off open-top bus tours are a good way to see the city. The only operator is Belfast City Sightseeing (tel: 028-9032 1321; www.belfastcitysightseeing.com; daily 10am–4pm). The tour begins on Castle Place and takes in all the sights, including Titanic Belfast, Stormont, the Botanic Gardens, Queens University and the murals on the Falls and Shankill roads. Kids colouring packs are available on-board.

A debt to St Paul's

The City Hall's design, freely appropriated from St Paul's Cathedral in London, has been dubbed 'Wrenaissance' but is deemed 'Classical Renaissance' by its admirers. Like a giant wedding cake, a copper Ionic dome rises to

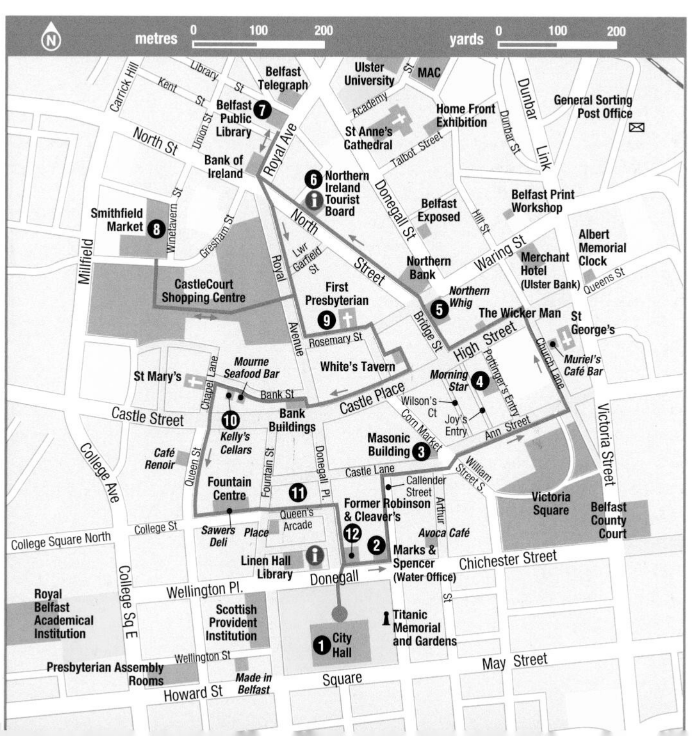

The copper-coated domes of City Hall.

Stained-glass windows inside City Hall trace Belfast's industrial past.

173ft (53m) above the centre. Two storeys of a Portland stone quadrangle, each corner equipped with a tower, surround a central courtyard.

In front stands Thomas Brock's statue of Queen Victoria. Victoria's back is to the pediment portico and its curious tomb-like porte-cochere, suggesting Her Majesty, unamused, has stepped out of her mausoleum.

Inside, an ornate Carrara marble staircase sweeps up from the marble grandiloquence of the Entrance Hall to the Rotunda, colonnaded in Cipollino marble. Off this are the Reception Room, Banqueting Hall and Council Chamber. Above the Rotunda, under the Great Dome, is the whispering gallery and John Luke's mural, commissioned to mark the 1951 Festival of Britain, illustrating the foundation of the city and the industries that provided its wealth. The striking Great

City Hall Gardens

Statues commemorate various worthies, from frock-coated mayors to James Magennis, a working-class Catholic from the Belfast slums who was the only Northern Ireland recipient of the Victoria Cross during World War II. In 1995 President Bill Clinton addressed huge crowds during a hopeful phase of the peace process, near a column recalling the first European touchdown of the US Expeditionary Force, who disembarked here on 26 January 1942.

Sitting with the statues in City Hall Gardens.

Hall (rebuilt after German bombing in 1941) has its original seven stained-glass windows, depicting three monarchs who have visited Belfast (William III, Victoria and Edward VII), and the shields of Ireland's four provinces.

GRAND ARCHITECTURE

Across Donegall Square North, east from the City Hall gates, the influence of Lanyon's firm crops up again in a red sandstone four-storey Venetian Gothic mass, completed in 1869 as a linen warehouse. This later became the Water Office until magisterially restored by **Marks & Spencer ❷**, the carved vegetable frieze suiting their business. On New Year's Day 1884, Oscar Wilde proclaimed this to be the city's sole beautiful building.

Beside M&S, and taking its name from callendering, a smoothing process for linen, Callender Street was once an alleyway for the businesses of distilling and newspaper publishing, now a short cut through to pedestrianised Castle Lane. Turn right on Castle Lane, where five streets converge on Arthur Square. Note the Art Nouveau detailing on the 1906 Mayfair Building and the 1870 **Masonic Building ❸**, Nos 13–21, also by Lanyon's firm and standing on the site of oyster houses, a trade that prospered down William Street South. Here in 1875, from the still attractive Nos 13–

The decorative marble interior of City Hall.

Pottinger's Entry, the historical narrow alleyway.

19, William Ross planned wells 420ft (130m) deep to obtain pure water for his celebrated Belfast Ginger Ale. Centuries back, Donegalls moored their pleasure barges in what is now Arthur Street, which branches out from here, and the Corn Market was an active spot. Arthur Street now has two highlights, the stylish Irish homeware, clothes and gift shop Avoca, with its popular food hall and café (see page 37), and the sumptuous Parisian music hall-style Café Vaudeville (tel: 028-9043 9160; www.cafevaudeville.com), delightfully restored.

ANN STREET ENTRIES

In Ann Street, around the corner, a traditional local business, boot-making, continues through a number of cut-price shoe shops. The 1798 Presbyterian leader Henry Joy McCracken was held at No. 13 when it served as the Artillery Barracks, before he was hanged in the Corn Market.

However, our interest lies in nipping in and out of the quarter's narrow pub-lined entries, to your left heading north. From **Joy's Entry** (the third along) in 1737 the revolutionary martyr's grandfather Francis Joy established what is now the oldest continuously published newspaper in the English language, the *Belfast News Letter*. Its current rival, the *Irish News*, originally the *Morning News*, was first published in 1853 at No. 6 Crown Entry, the first entry you reach. The Society of United Irishmen was inaugurated in the Crown Tavern here in 1791. From **Wilson's Court**, between the two, the first edition of the United Irishmen's own newspaper, the *Northern Star*, was published.

Next, duck underneath a painted brick archway into **Pottinger's Entry** (see box), past the ornate **Morning Star** ❹ where Mary Ann McCracken attempted to revive her brother, having first bribed the hangman. It is the last of the area's celebrated oyster houses. Still with its original facade and a wonderful horseshoe bar, it was once a sailors' pub, at the start of the Dublin Coach route. Today, it's known for its old-school charm and excellent food.

The Pottingers

Pottinger's Entry is named after a prominent local family who supplied the city with gold sovereigns and the British army with moustached majors. The most noted of the family was Sir Henry Pottinger, who as the first governor of Hong Kong successfully negotiated the British lease of Hong Kong after the Chinese Opium Wars. He died in retirement on the island of Malta.

The acclaimed landscape water colourist and printmaker Andrew Nicholl (1804–86) was a boot-maker's son from Church Lane, the next road on the left. A blue plaque at No. 10 marks his birthplace. Next door is the delightfully bohemian **Muriel's Café Bar** (tel: 028-9033 2445). A few doors down, at No. 4, is an atmospheric old tobacconist, Miss Moran Ltd, named after the woman who owned it from the 1930s to 1980s.

HIGH STREET AND NORTH STREET

At the junction with High Street glance across the road at the Bank of Ireland – once the National Bank – where octagonal fish-scale turrets surmount a facade carved with centaurs and cornucopias. Turning west onto High Street, the tour follows the line of the Farset River, which still flows beneath it. Here lived the McCracken family and Sir James Murray, the innovator of Milk of Magnesia.

As you make your way around High Street you will come across several one-of-a-kind shops. **The Wicker Man** (tel: 028-9024 3550; www.thewickerman.co.uk) showcases top-of-the-range Irish and Celtic crafts. The shop is at Nos. 44–46 High Street on the ground floor of River House.

Take the next right into Bridge Street, past a grey 1960s building housing an uninspiring shopping centre which, somewhat bafflingly, has been listed. A bit further on you'll see the stylish **Northern Whig** ❺ on the corner of Waring Street at one entrance to the Cathedral Quarter (see page 48). Dating from 1819, the building has housed a hotel and newspaper offices (of the same name) and is now a Soviet-themed pub with a good all-day menu. A forerunner of the stylish bars that have proliferated, it remains one of its most enjoyable.

To the north, North Street, having been much redeveloped over recent decades, struggles to keep its once-interesting character. On the corner of Lower Garfield Street stands the Victorian Deer's Head pub, which still has five of its original snugs and serves good traditional Irish food. At St Anne's Court the **Northern Ireland Tourist Board** ❻ (entrance around the corner on Writer's Square) deals with tourist information and bookings.

ROYAL AVENUE

Around the corner, in Royal Avenue, the city's main shopping thoroughfare

Stopping for a pint at The Morning Star.

A colourful mural inside Smithfield Market.

since Victorian times, you will find the French-looking three-storey **Belfast Public Library** ❼ (tel: 028-9050 9150; Mon and Thu 9am–8pm, Tue, Wed and Fri until 5.30pm, Sat 10am–4.30pm), in red sandstone, designed by Lanyon's partner Lynn and completed in 1888. For those wishing to research Belfast or Northern Irish history and culture, this is a good place to start, with a wide range of periodicals and newspapers going back to the 19th century.

Next door stands the office of the *Belfast Telegraph*, one of Northern Ireland's three daily newspapers. Although generally perceived as reflecting a moderate unionism, it is owned these days by a Catholic, Tony O'Reilly, as part of his Independent empire embracing newspapers in London, Dublin and South Africa.

Now the route turns on its head to journey back down Royal Avenue towards Donegall Place and City Hall. Standing on a corner site at the junction with North Street, you can't miss the Bank of Ireland, a fabulous Art Deco building featuring a central clock, and considered by many to be the best modern building in Belfast. The Albert, Gresham and Crown chambers, also on the right, retain some of their period charm, as do Donegall, Eagle, Royal and Avenue chambers on the left.

The reflective glass and stainless steel of **Castle Court shopping centre** (tel: 028-9023 4591; www.castlecourt-uk.com) reflects its confidence as one of the city's best, with numerous top high-street names among its 80 retail outlets. Until the 1960s this was the site of the Grand Central Hotel. Later its grand rooms were converted into a British Army base.

In Winetavern Street, at the back of Castle Court, stands **Smithfield Market** ❽ on the site of the famous

Victorian market. The mall sells a range of goods including comics, camping equipment and model soldiers. Retrace your steps through the shopping centre to Royal Avenue.

ROSEMARY STREET

Our route diverts east into Rosemary Street where in 1785 Sarah Siddons, the celebrated actress, played at its long-gone 18th-century Playhouse, just opposite the delightful **First Presbyterian Church** ❾. Dating from 1781, this is the city's oldest surviving place of worship. Its interior is boat-like and elliptical, its woodwork divine, its ceiling radically plastered, its pews boxed. Such was the fervour of dogma among 18th-century Dissenters that splits led them to build two further churches, since demolished, in the same street.

The route turns right into Lombard Street, from which the Irish Temperance League once operated, then smartly left again into the courtyard of Winecellar Entry, past the upturned cannon-barrel bollards to the atmospheric **White's Tavern**, associated with the wine trade since 1630 but much rebuilt. A further right turn in this dingy canyon brings you back to High Street. Turn right again and head west into Castle Place, where little remains that would suggest its former Victorian commercial focus as a place of silk merchants and tea shops. Where the former Donegall Arcade (now home to a T.K. Maxx outlet) stands was once the Provost Prison where those to be hanged were held. Only W.H. Lynn's five-storey red sandstone **Bank Buildings**, directly in front (now occupied by Primark), and the Victorian and Art Nouveau detail high up on Castle Buildings at Nos 8–18, give a flavour of past times.

Cross over Royal Avenue and leave the Bank Buildings on your left, but not before popping into the Tesco Metro store that inhabits the former Provincial Bank building. Designed by W.J. Barre, it has a stunning ornate glazed dome.

OFF THE MAIN ROUTE

Tucked behind here, Bank Street runs west to **Kelly's Cellars** ❿, a pub established in 1720 and retaining some of the conspiratorial ambiance generated when Henry Joy McCracken crouched beneath the counter escaping the Redcoats. A left turn leads us to Chapel Lane opposite **St Mary's Roman**

Fresh Garbage

You are unlikely to overlook the vivid facade and signage of Fresh Garbage at 24 Rosemary Street (tel: 028-9024 2350), an absolute treasure trove for anyone looking for interesting second-hand clothes, jewellery and other items, ranging in style from hippy to rock, punk and grunge.

Catholic Chapel, whose walls date from 1783 and whose original opening was formally and ecumenically saluted by the Presbyterians of the 1st Belfast Volunteer Company. Cross over Castle Street at the junction, with the 1865 Hercules Bar on the corner into Queen Street and here you'll find the excellent Café Renoir, some evangelical faith shops and arts and crafts stores.

COLLEGE STREET TO DONEGALL PLACE

At College Street head east, where there are a number of shops worthy of investigation. The **Bradbury Art Gallery** (3 Lyndon Court; tel: 028-9023 8450; www.bradburyart.co.uk) has regular exhibitions of contemporary art, numerous special events and a well-stocked shop.

The 'Alice Clock' at the **Fountain Centre**, is Ireland's only automaton clock, with a curious procession of characters from *Alice in Wonderland* and the Nativity. Utopia (tel: 028 9024 1342; www.utopiabelfast.com) is a wonderful gift shop with something for all ages.

Shopping in Queen's Arcade.

On the ground floor of the Fountain Centre, Sawers (tel: 028-9032 2021; www.sawersbelfast.com) is a traditional Belfast deli with excellent local fish and seafood delicacies (potted herring and smoked Irish wild salmon) and a staggering 150 Irish and international cheeses.

Back on Fountain Street, call into Place (028-9023 2524; www.placeni.org) at No. 40, an architectural centre where you can learn more about the city's built heritage. They organise guided walking tours of the city centre, as well as exhibitions and other events.

The 1880s-built **Queen's Arcade** ⓫, largely inhabited by jewellery shops, leads us back to the busy thoroughfare of Donegall Place. Above Queen's Arcade Buildings take note of the Disneyesque maquette of Belfast Castle. On the east side of Donegall Place, your eyes will also be led upwards to eight maritime copper masts installed in 2011 and now an established part of central Belfast's cityscape. Each of the illuminated curved masts represents a ship from the White Star Line series built by Harland and Wolff.

Robinson & Cleaver

Now colonised almost entirely by British high-street multiples, on the other side of Donegall Place stands what was once the province's leading store, still bearing the name of **Robinson & Cleaver** ⓬. Originally a linen warehouse, this six-storey building boasts a clock tower, a flock of Donatello cherubs and 50 stone heads of those claimed as the firm's patrons, plus symbolic references to far-flung marketplaces. It also houses a deli and restaurant also called Robinson & Cleaver (tel: 028 9031 2538; www.robinsonandcleaver.com) with great views over City Hall and back to where you started.

Robinson & Cleaver.

Eating Out

Avoca Café
41 Arthur Street; tel: 028-9027 9955; www.avoca.com; Mon–Sat 9am–5pm, Sun 1–5pm.
The upstairs restaurant serves the usual eclectic food and great baking for which the Irish retail family Avoca is renowned. Favourites include their traditional beef and Guinness casserole. ££

Made in Belfast
1–2 Wellington Buildings, Wellington Street; tel: 028-9024 6712; www.madeinbelfastni.com; Mon–Thu noon–9.30pm, Fri–Sat until 10pm, Sun until 9pm.
Funky and fun, this buzzy restaurant is tucked down a side street beside the City Hall. Dishes range from whole-baked Irish Cooleeny cheese with homemade fougasse loaf to steamed Strangford Lough rope-grown mussels and beefburgers topped with Irish Cheddar cheese and beef-fat chips. ££

The Morning Star
17–19 Pottinger's Entry; tel: 028-9023 5986; www.themorningstarbar.com; Mon–Wed noon–9pm, Thu–Sat until 10pm, Sun until 5pm.
A historic traditional pub well hidden down a narrow entry. Inside and up the steep staircase is a classic Belfast dining experience combining quality ingredients with the motto 'grown here, not flown here'. ££

Mourne Seafood Bar
34–6 Bank Street; tel: 028-9024 8544; www.mourneseafood.com; Mon–Thu noon–9.30pm, Fri–Sat noon–4pm and 5–10.30pm, Sun 1–9pm.
Top of the list for seafood lovers. Fresh seafood, sourced from the restaurant's shellfish beds, is cooked in a traditional style or with an Asian twist. Make your way up to the Oyster Bar for a cheaper alternative to the main dining room where the menu features small plates. ££

The Northern Whig
2–10 Bridge Street; tel: 028-9050 9888; www.thenorthernwhig.com; food served daily noon–9pm.
Formerly home to the newspaper of the same name, this bar has been restored with a Soviet theme to provide a chic, relaxed spot for dining. Leave room for the hot-chocolate ganache pudding which the locals rave about. £–££

Stix & Stones
44–46 Upper Queen Street; tel: 028-9031 9418; www.stixandstones belfast.co.uk; Mon–Fri noon–3pm, 5–10pm, Sat 1–3pm, 5–10pm, Sun 4–9pm.
This hugely popular restaurant specialises in the diner cooking their own steak or seafood on hot stones in a casual, laid-back restaurant, with live music on Saturday nights. ££

Historic Pubs

Whether for its history, its *craic* (a good time/conversation) or its decor, a visit to one of the atmospheric old pubs in Belfast should feature on every visitor's itinerary.

Belfast's population explosion in the 18th century meant that, by the time Queen Victoria came to the throne in 1836, there were an impressive 346 public houses in the city, many offering accommodation and, later, musical entertainment. Today this profusion of pubs has dwindled, but some of the old inns have survived and are worth seeking out for the wealth of history concealed behind their doors. If you have the time, the easiest way to explore the best of the old-fashioned Belfast pubs is on a Historical Pubs Tour (tel. 028-9268 3665; www.belfastpubtours.com).

THE *CRAIC*

This peculiarly Irish term has always been more associated with Dublin than Belfast. It's taken a long time to break down this misconception, but the signs are that more and more visitors are coming to Belfast precisely for its growing reputation for the *craic*.

PICK OF THE BEST

The oldest

McHugh's (see page 67), in what is claimed to be Belfast's oldest building, has been skilfully renovated with exposed original brickwork and beams and a ship's boiler built into the walls. To mark its 300th anniversary, a spe-

Strumming at Bittles Bar.

cially brewed McHughs 300 beer has been produced by the Whitewater Brewery in Kilkeel, County Down.

Established in 1720, **Kelly's Cellars** (30–32 Bank Street; tel 028-9024 4835; www.kellyscellars.com) has attracted a fair share of bohemians and revolutionaries in its time and still has an interesting mix of clientele.

An ancient pub with an old-world feel is **White's Tavern** (2–4 Winecellar Entry; tel: 028-9024 3080; www.whitesbelfast.com) down a cobblestoned entry. Retro films are screened in the courtyard cinema. Upstairs is the self-styled 'geek and movie bar' Vandal (tel: 028-9031 2582; www.vandalbelfast.co.uk), which serves excellent pizza and hosts games nights.

The Morning Star (see page 37), hidden down Pottinger's Entry, a former terminal for the Belfast–Dublin mail coach, has been beautifully restored.

Victorian gems

The jewel in the crown of Victorian Belfast pubs is the **Crown Liquor Saloon** (see page 22). It may be more self-conscious of its tourist appeal these days, but don't ignore its delightful craftsmanship – exquisite tile and glass work – and atmospheric snugs.

The Garrick Bar (29 Chichester Street; tel: 028-9033 3875; www.thegarrickbar.com) is a nicely restored old lawyers' pub.

Another pub that has retained its decorative Victorian interior is **Aether & Echo** (1–3 Lower Garfield Street; tel: 028-9023 9163; http://aetherandecho.com).

Literary connections

The Duke of York (7 Commercial Court; tel: 028-9024 1062; www.dukeofyorkbelfast.com) is a former journalists' pub (though most famous for its former barman, now Sinn Féin leader, Gerry Adams) and retains an old-fashioned intimacy.

The John Hewitt (51 Donegall Street; tel: 028-9023 3768; www.thejohnhewitt.com), named after the Belfast poet, has a strong cultural flavour and features literary events.

Bittles Bar (70 Upper Church Lane; tel: 028-9031 1088) is a distinctive triangular pub with a literary feel. You will encounter pictures of a large assortment of Ireland's literary giants, from Wilde to Joyce, on the walls of its tri-cornered lounge.

St Anne's Cathedral.

Tour 3

Cathedral Quarter

At just over a mile (2km) and taking half a day, this circular tour around the Cathedral Quarter has plenty to offer.

CULTURAL REVIVAL

The opening of the luxurious Merchant Hotel in 2006 gave a massive impetus to Belfast's much vaunted new cultural area, the Cathedral Quarter. By the 1990s, the area had fallen into disrepair and, given that a good proportion of its Victorian buildings remained, it was considered the best location to create a mixed artistic, commercial and entertainment district. The regeneration of this area is a huge success story and it has become the hub of a thriving social scene. It stepped up another level in 2012 with the completion of the Metropolitan Arts Centre (MAC) along with a clutch of new restaurants and a hotel in Saint Anne's Square. Revitalised red-bricked buildings house small galleries showcasing the work of sculptors and photographers as well as installation artists. Potter around the tight network of cobbled streets and you will feel the modern vibe: old pubs rub shoulders with cool hotels while wine bars and stylish bistros are found down narrow alleyways.

Highlights

- Royal Ulster Rifles Museum
- Merchant Hotel
- The MAC
- The Black Box
- Home Front Exhibition
- St Patrick's RC Church
- St Anne's Cathedral

The Cloth Ear.

WARING STREET

We begin the route where Bridge Street meets Waring Street. Opposite the popular Northern Whig pub is another excellent building, the original 1769 Exchange and Assembly Rooms, converted to a bank, the **Northern**, by Lanyon in 1845. Italianate stucco, the architect's trademark, is everywhere. In 1792 the premises hosted the famous Harp Festival, during which the young musicologist Edward Bunting transcribed the traditional airs and compositions of the last of this island's blind harpers.

Across Donegall Arcade, after years of neglect, the lovely facade of the Four Corners building now fronts a Premier Inn Hotel. Worth visiting on Waring Street at No. 5 (just before the 1998 Peace Mural), the **Royal Ulster Rifles Museum** ❶ (tel: 028-9023 2086; Tue–Fri 10am–4pm; free) has an extensive collection of regimental memorabilia and traces the regiment back to 1793.

Further on, a slight detour south to Skipper Street (which provided lodging for tea-clipper skippers) brings us to a delightful bar, The Spaniard at No. 3, which offers wine and tapas as well as a selection of Havana cocktails such as Mai tai and Havana Sours.

Arts festival

Much of the success of the area in establishing a cultural identity has been down to a well-regarded alternative arts festival, the Cathedral Quarter Arts Festival, which each May brings a wide variety of Irish and international artists to venues throughout the quarter.

Returning to Waring Street, on the corner is the Ulster Buildings, housing the **Cloth Ear** restaurant (see page 47), a solid 1869 sandstone block. Opposite is the startling cubic frontage of a three-storey building on the site of a 17th-century pot-house, its history reflected in the use of materials – stone, wood, glass and cobblestones – to construct the new building (2004), a luxury hotel. This was the site of William Waring's home, a tanner, for whom the street was named. His daughter, Jane, grew up to become Dean Jonathan Swift's Varina, refusing to marry him while he was prebendary at Kilroot, near Carrickfergus, in 1696.

Next door, Cotton Court is an old bonded warehouse. It is home to an ec-

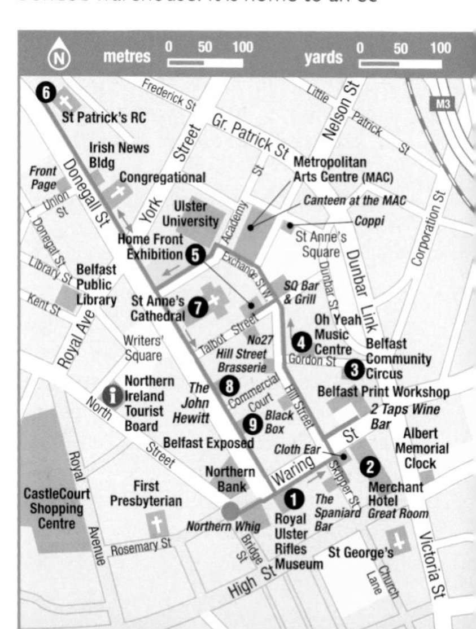

The sumptuous Great Room restaurant, in the Merchant Hotel, is situated in the former main Banking Hall of the building.

lectic mix, including the **Belfast Print Workshop** (tel: 028-9023 1323; www.bpw.org.uk), which provides facilities for artists who work in printmaking to share ideas and create original prints. They can then sell their work in Northern Ireland's first original print gallery. It also houses **Craft NI** (tel: 028-9032 3059; www.craftni.org), which has good exhibitions of ceramics, textiles and other work. Peruse the huge tiled mural filling an entire wall and you will discover that it reflects the historic trades that were carried out in Waring Street: tea merchants, saddlers, linen and damask manufacturers, millers, shirt makers, and marine engineering.

MERCHANT HOTEL

On the other side of the road stands the street's final distinctive building, the 1860s former Ulster Bank, now the **Merchant Hotel** ❷ (see page 125), with an elaborate cast-iron balustrade and extravaganza of Thomas Fitzpatrick's carvings. The skyline is dominated by his figures of Britannia, Justice and Commerce, and urns surmount the corners. The Grade A listed building was bought and restored at enormous cost by Beannchor, which runs various Belfast restaurants and bars. It opened in 2006 as the Merchant, and quickly established itself as Northern Ireland's premier luxury hotel.

The hotel radiates wealth, not least in the spectacular **Great Room** restaurant (see page 47), where Ireland's largest chandelier hangs beneath a glass cupola. In 2010 the hotel added a sleek £16-million extension which includes a luxury spa and rooftop gym

The MAC

The MAC (Metropolitan Arts Centre, St Anne's Square; 028–9023 5053; www.themaclive.com; daily 10am–7pm; free) is Belfast's newest arts venue. It comes with two theatres, three art galleries and artists' studios, along with a café, bar and restaurant. With its red brick and dark basalt, as well as oak furnishings, Danish fabric panels, steel balustrades and bronze window frames, it has caught the imagination of locals and visitors alike, exceeding all expectations and justifying the £18m cost of building.

with panoramic views of the city. Bert's Jazz Bar is also a fashionable spot for authentic live music (daily) in Art Deco surroundings.

HILL STREET

Diagonally opposite the hotel, with its many hidden courtyards (their corners protected from carriage wheels by heavy iron bollards) and some listed brick and stucco warehouses, the cobblestoned **Hill Street** typifies the promise that earned the area its regeneration. At Nos 18–22 the **Black Box** auditorium (tel: 028-9024 4400; www.blackboxbelfast.com) stages live music, drama, comedy, exhibitions, science festivals and cabaret. It also offers street art walking tours of the Cathedral Quarter.

Just off Hill Street on the right, at 23–25 Gordon Street is one of the quarter's more unusual stars, the **Belfast Community Circus** ❸ (tel: 028-9023 6007; www.belfastcircus.org), housed in a suitably brightly coloured building. Classes are available from two years of age upwards. The accomplished artistes perform throughout the year, from special days at St George's Market to numerous City Council events and at the venue's cabaret nights. Biggest of all is their own Festival of Fools in May, with trapeze artists, acrobats and wire-walkers in action on the streets.

Staying on Gordon Street, at Nos 15–21 you may be drawn in by the strains of *Brown Eyed Girl* ringing in your

Looking out over the atrium at the MAC.

The glistening steel spire of St Anne's Cathedral.

ears. The lyrics of Belfast's most famous musical son, Van Morrison, emanate from the **Oh Yeah Music Centre** ❹ (tel: 028-9031 0845; www.ohyeahbelfast.com; Mon–Fri 10am–4pm; free). This converted warehouse hosts a music exhibition, rehearsal space, café, and recording studio, as well as events such as an 'acoustic picnic' with activities for children, food and live

School of Art and Design, Ulster University.

music. Return to Hill Street and continue to the end.

SAINT ANNE'S SQUARE

Divert left to visit the **Home Front Exhibition** ❺ at 21 Talbot Street, (tel: 028-9032 0392; www.niwarmemorial.org; Mon–Fri 10.30am–4.30pm, June–Sept also Sun 11am–1pm; free). Part of the Northern Ireland War Memorial, the exhibition gives an in-depth account of Northern Ireland during World War II, with photos, artefacts and interactive exhibits.

Return to Hill Street now and cross over to **Saint Anne's Square**, which runs behind the Protestant St Anne's Cathedral. The highlight of this neo-Palladian development is the MAC, Northern Ireland's new flagship home for the arts (see page 43). Surrounding the square are blocks of smart porticoed apartments sitting alongside half a dozen trendy restaurants serving everything from modern Irish and Italian to contemporary Chinese cuisine.

BACK TO DONEGALL STREET

Leaving the pleasing rear view of the 1901 cathedral building on the left, cross the square in front of the £35-million redevelopment of the Ulster University Art School, completed in 2008. The street here is known as **Academy Street**, so-called after David Manson's 1768 co-educational establishment. Despite regulations forbidding dogs and guns, nine pupils at No. 2 (now demolished but once the Belfast Academy) took their masters hostage at gunpoint when they heard Easter Holidays were to be cancelled. No. 40, built as a distiller's warehouse, now houses the Belfast Education and Library Board. Join up with Donegall Street and head northwest up towards St Patrick's Church. At No. 90 stands **The Kremlin** (tel. 028-9031

Financing St Patrick's

In the early 19th century Catholics accounted for one-sixth of Belfast's population and numbers grew as people came to the city to work in the new industries. A plot of ground was leased in 1809 from the marquis of Donegall for a new church. Of the £4,100 raised to finance St Patrick's construction, £1,300 was subscribed by Protestants – an indication that the two communities were not always at each other's throats.

6060; www.kremlin-belfast.com), one of Belfast's most popular and best-known gay venues, with three separate levels, amazing themed nights and a legendary nightclub. On the opposite side of the road, down from the *Irish News* offices, is a 1932 reconstruction of the German Blitz-damaged 1860 sandstone of **Donegall Street Congregational Church**.

ST PATRICK'S

John Willis, first organist at the 1815 Gothic Revivalist **St Patrick's Roman Catholic Church** ❻ beyond, was dismissed almost as soon as he was engaged for playing variations on *The Boyne Water*, a belligerent Orange Protestant marching tune, at a service. The side chapel triptych of St Patrick, the Madonna and St Bridget is by the society painter and war artist Sir John Lavery. The Madonna's face is that of Lavery's wife Hazel, said by her husband to have influenced her friend, Irish revolutionary Michael Collins, to sign the Anglo-Irish treaty of 1921 that ushered in partition.

Next to the church, St Patrick's School is of an even earlier vintage (1828) and was the first Catholic school to be built in Belfast. The elegant three-storey houses to the north have been restored, making them among the earliest block of domestic premises to survive in the city.

The exterior of St Patrick's Roman Catholic Church.

ST ANNE'S CATHEDRAL

Retrace your steps south to the main facade of **St Anne's Cathedral** ❼. Pause here and reflect on **Writers' Square** opposite, a public space which contains sculptural pieces by John Kindness and Brian Connolly. It is also used as a venue for street performers and festival events, including the Festival of Fools and the Cathedral Quarter Arts Festival each May.

View from the spire

In 2007 a futuristic 131ft (40m) stainless-steel spire was installed on the top of St Anne's Cathedral. Known as the Spire of Hope, it affords several excellent views from both the outside and inside of the cathedral. The base of the spire protrudes through a glass platform directly above the choir stalls, enabling visitors to look up at it from the nave. Illuminated at night, the spire can be seen as a beacon of hope in the Cathedral Quarter.

Inside St Anne's Cathedral.

A neo-Romanesque construction of Portland stone, begun in 1898, St Anne's only added its stainless-steel spire in 2007 (see page 45). It succeeds a previous parish church, named as much after Anne, wife of the fifth earl of Donegall, as after Mary's mother. The rather plain nave's spaciousness is due in part to it being built around its predecessor, where services were held until 1903. The pulpit, designed by Gilbert Scott, was carved by Harry Hems. Impressive features include a tympanum filled with a mosaic of angel musicians on a background of gold, one of Ireland's largest church organs, and delightful stained-glass windows. The baptistery has a ceiling made of 150,000 pieces of glass, representing the basic elements of creation. In 2012, as part of the Titanic centennial commemorations, an elegant *Titanic* Funeral Pall was unveiled.

Time for a tipple at the Duke of York in Commercial Court.

THE REST OF DONEGALL STREET

Continue south down Donegall Street to one of Belfast's most culturally lively pubs, the community-run **John Hewitt** ❽ (tel: 028-9023 3768; www.thejohnhewitt.com) at No. 51. Named after a famous local poet, it maintains an atmospheric feel. Food is of a high gastro-pub standard, and the music – traditional jazz and blues – is excellent. It is a hub of activity during festival time.

Just off Donegall Street is pretty Commercial Court (which we saw from the other end on Hill Street). Here the Duke of York (tel: 028-9024 1062; www.dukeofyorkbelfast.com) was a hacks' pub where Gerry Adams, president of Sinn Féin, worked as a barman in the 1960s. Today it's better known for a strong roster of music throughout the week.

Back on Donegall Street, No. 23 houses **Belfast Exposed** ❾ (tel: 028-9023 0965), Northern Ireland's only dedicated photographic gallery, which has a large archive of digital images. It also includes the offices of the Belfast Film Festival (tel: 028-9032 5913, www.belfastfilmfestival.org), which takes place in April, with a programme of premieres, classics and short-film competitions. Their Visions Studio also has a programme of digital screenings throughout the year. Northern Visions (tel: 028-9024 5495; www.nvtv.co.uk), a community media and arts project that broadcasts a local TV channel, is also here.

Continue to the end of Donegall Street and you arrive back at the start of the walk.

Eating Out

2 Taps Wine Bar
Cotton Court, 42 Waring Street; tel: 028-9031 1414; www.2taps-winebar.co.uk; Tue–Wed and Sun noon–8.30pm, Thu until 9pm, Fri–Sat until 10.30pm.
A taste of Spain in the heart of Belfast. Relax in the pleasant warm dining room or eat alfresco on the heated outdoor terrace. Meat, fish and vegetarian tapas, fresh salads and paella made to order are among the Spanish specialities. ££

The Cloth Ear
The Merchant Hotel, 35–9 Waring Street; tel: 028-9026 2719; www.themerchanthotel.com; Mon–Sat noon–9pm, Sun 12.30–9pm.
A good all-round menu makes this a perfect stop in the Cathedral Quarter. Its food is advertised as 'home comfort', with the sharing roasts on Sundays proving particularly popular. Its ambience is warm and its decor features deer's heads. ££

Coppi
St Anne's Square; tel: 028-9031 1959; www.coppi.co.uk; Mon–Thu and Sun noon–10pm, Fri–Sat until 11pm.
This contemporary restaurant is named after Fausto Coppi, an Italian cyclist from the mid-20th century. You can sample *cichetti* (Venetian tapas) with a glass of Prosecco or delicious lamb and pomegranate pizzettas. For more substantial dishes, choose from monkfish, steak Florentine or risotto and mushroom puff. ££

The Great Room
The Merchant Hotel, 35–9 Waring Street; tel: 028-9026 2719; www.themerchanthotel.com; breakfast Mon–Fri 7–10am, Sat–Sun 7.30–10.30am, lunch Mon–Sat noon–2.30pm, 3–5.30pm, dinner Mon–Sat 6–8.30pm, 9pm–late, Sun menu 12.30–8pm.
If you are not too blown away by the splendid dining room, the international menu here is a treat. The signature dish is traditional beef Wellington, its presentation far from ordinary. Also a good bet for scrumptious afternoon tea. Recommended for special occasions. £££

NATIVE at the Mac
10 Exchange Street West; tel: 028-9023 5053; www.themaclive.com; daily 10am–7pm; last orders extended until 7.30pm on performance nights.
NATIVE is an ideal spot to take a break on your cultural tour of Belfast's glitziest arts venue. The all-day menu includes roasted hake fillet with chorizo crust and butterbean stew. The 'Bites' menu features smaller versions of the mains for only £3.50 a pop. £

OX
1 Oxford Street; tel: 028-9031 4121; http://oxbelfast.com; lunch Tue–Fri noon–2.30pm, Sat 1–2.30pm; dinner Tue–Sat 6–9.30pm.
Since opening in 2013, OX quickly won the accolade of Belfast's best fine-dining experience from critics and diners alike. Its no-choice tasting menu offers fare such as chateaubriand with foie gras or turbot with coral butter, Romanesco and lemongrass. £££

SQ Bar & Grill
Ramada Encore Belfast City Centre, St Anne's Square; tel: 028-9026 1809; www.sqbarandgrill.co.uk; breakfast Mon–Fri 6.30–10am, Sat–Sun 7–10.30am, lunch/dinner daily noon–9.45pm.
The grill is located in the Ramada Hotel overlooking Saint Anne's Square. Local ingredients are given a modern twist to create some interesting dishes, including five-hour braised daube of beef and pan-fried monkfish. ££

The Crescent Arts Centre.

Tour 4

Queen's Quarter

Based around Sir Charles Lanyon's Queen's University, this 2-mile (3km) half-day walk is a mixture of student haunts, elegant academia and shopping heaven.

A genteel area, one of Belfast's more rewarding for lovers of Victorian and Edwardian architecture, **Queen's Quarter** also has lively student pubs and stylish bars, numerous ethnic restaurants, art galleries, boutique hotels and budget hostels and Belfast's best-known road for fashion hunting. The autumnal Belfast International Arts Festival, focused on Queen's, is the biggest in the UK after Edinburgh, and makes an excellent introduction to the city for the first-time visitor as it utilises so many venues around Belfast.

Highlights

- Crescent Arts Centre and Gardens
- Lisburn Road shops
- Queen's University
- Ulster Museum
- Botanic Gardens

BRADBURY PLACE

Start in Bradbury Place, just south of Shaftesbury Square, where during the 1950s and 1960s **Lavery's Gin Palace** ❶ (Nos 12–16; tel: 028-9087 1106; www.laverysbelfast.com) was a haven for artists and poets, including William Conor, John Hewitt and Louis MacNeice. It now offers a wide range of live music throughout the week, from reggae to folk. The newest addition is the Woodworkers Rotating Tap Bar, serving specialist craft beer. On the top floor is Northern Ireland's largest pool room, with 22 pool tables opening out onto the roof terraces.

Shop till you drop

Along the 1-mile (1.6km) length of Lisburn Road you will find more than 100 independent businesses providing an unparalleled range of shops, from boutiques displaying the latest designer names and more quirky styles, to galleries, antique shops and contemporary homeware stores, complemented by a wide choice of restaurants, bars and delis to tempt hungry shoppers.

At No. 10 Bradbury Place is Darcy's (tel. 028-9032 4040; www.darcysbelfast.co.uk), a family-run restaurant with a great vegetarian menu. Across the road at Nos 23–31 is Alibi (tel. 028-9023 3131; http://alibibelfast.com), a nightclub, cocktail bar and grill over three levels. At Nos 7–21, Benedict's Hotel (tel: 028-9059 1999; www.benedictshotel.co.uk) is a three-star hotel with a popular bar, with live music some nights until the early hours, and a restaurant.

A lengthy detour from Bradbury Place, taking the right fork along the long Lisburn Road (see box), will take dedicated shoppers to one of Belfast's prime retail districts interspersed with great places to eat; it's a hive of activity day and night.

At the junction of Lisburn Road and Bradbury Place is tiny **King William Park**, commemorated in Frank Ormsby's eponymous ironic poem, where William III hitched his horse in 1690. Note the pinnacle spire of the 1887 Moravian church and the campanile of the Wesleyan chapel, designed by W. J. Barre, which would not look out of place in Lombardy.

THE CRESCENTS

Further south, past an octagonal Art Deco weathercock-topped gazebo at No. 48 and over the railway bridge, into the University Conservation Area, the 1873 Scrabo stone baronial pile that is the **Crescent Arts Centre** ❷ (2–4 University Road; tel: 028-9024 2338; www.crescentarts.org), stands at the corner of University Road and Lower Crescent. This maze of rooms and studios plays host to a huge variety of regular workshops and classes in all aspects of the arts, to an acclaimed midsummer dance festival and the annual Belfast Book Festival held in June (www.belfastbookfestival.com).

The Crescent Centre's neighbour is the **Crescent Church**, charismatic in its worship and French medieval in its architectural inspiration. Our route nips east behind the church past the grand pilasters of the stuccoed Georgian terraces of Lower Crescent and the pleasant **Crescent Gardens** ❸ (once a potato patch), with a stop for a pint at the Fly (5–6 Lower Crescent

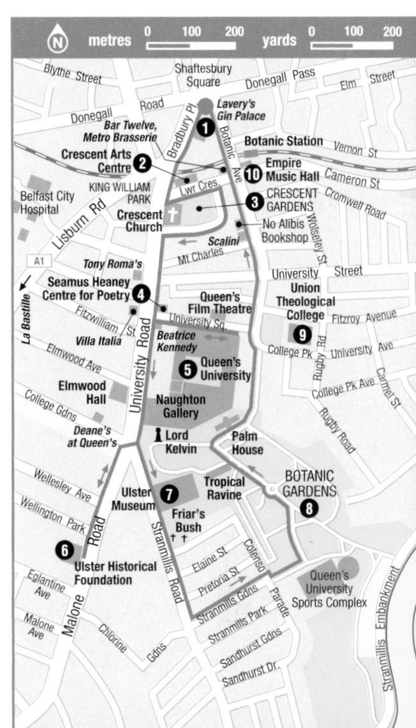

Gardens; tel: 028-9050 9750), a student hotspot where a heady mix of sport and music is the focus of attention. At No. 13 is one of the city's earliest boutique hotels, the three-star Crescent Townhouse (tel: 028-9032 3349; www.crescenttownhouse.com), a 19th-century building whose suites are bathed in period decor. Its excellent Town Square café (45 Botanic Ave; tel: 079-38 244 851; http://townsquarebelfast.com) serves breakfast until 2pm – perfect for a lazy Saturday morning catch-up over eggs benedict and hand-roasted coffee.

UNIVERSITY ROAD

Returning to imposing Upper Crescent and then University Road, we pass southwards to the pleasant stucco and Doric porticoes of Mount Charles, once home to novelist Forrest Reid and the poet John Hewitt.

Along University Road are a number of restaurants, ranging from a branch of the world-dominating rib specialist **Tony Roma's** (see page 54) to the ever-popular **Villa Italia** and local favourite **Buskers** (see page 54). Turn into Elmwood Avenue to find The Parlour bar at Nos 2–4 (tel: 028-9068 6970; www.parlourbar.co.uk). This 1930's themed student haunt serves mouth-watering pizza and hosts live music.

Across the road are three Georgian rows, Prospect Terrace, Botanic View and Cinnamond's Buildings, plus the Victorian stucco and Georgian brick terraces of Camden and Fitzwilliam streets. These, respectively, were the home ground of Brian Moore's 1956 novel *The Lonely Passion of Judith Hearne*, and the site of Nobel Laureate poet Seamus Heaney's campus flat.

Take a detour east down Georgian University Square to view several

Queen's campus

Queen's University campus is modest in size and so, as the university expanded to its present numbers of 24,000 students and 1,600 teaching and research staff, it began buying up every vacant building in the area. Currently it owns more than 250. A large proportion of students come from Northern Ireland and many of them go home to their families at weekends, so social activities are less extensive than one might expect.

Students take a break from lectures.

The Lanyon Building at Queen's University.

houses – now university departments – that sport magnolia in their gardens. At No. 1 is the **Seamus Heaney Centre for Poetry** ❹ (tel: 028-9097 1070), attached to the School of English at Queen's and a regular venue for literary talks and events of a consistently high calibre. At 20 University Square is the **Queen's Film Theatre**, the only place to catch the latest in world cinema in Belfast (tel: 028-9097 1097; www.queensfilmtheatre.com). It has two big screens, a theatre and a comfortable bar and lounge in which to debate the relative merits of Yasujiro Ozu and Quentin Tarantino.

Back on University Road, The Church of Ireland's Canon Hannay (1865–1950), aka George A. Birmingham, the nationalistic author of 60-plus satirical novels, lived at No. 75; painter Paul Henry lived at No. 61.

QUEEN'S UNIVERSITY

Charles Lanyon designed the pleasingly mellowed red-brick facade of **Queen's University** ❺ (see box), shamelessly appropriating the lines of the Founder's Tower at Magdalen College, Oxford, for its central feature. The university was named after the young Victoria when she laid the foundation stone in 1845. Adhering to the hierarchical nature of the times, the architect provided lavish accommodation for chancellors and other dignitaries while offering the students little except for four water closets and a row of urinals. Happily the new off-campus student village now compensates for this.

There are more than 100 listed buildings, dating back as far as 150 years, around the campus and surrounding area, and it's worth picking up the 'Walkabout Queen's' leaflet from the Queens Welcome Centre (tel: 028-9097 5252; Mon–Fri 8am–5pm) to help you on a signposted tour; enter the university's main gates and follow signs for the Welcome Centre. In particular, seek out the Great Hall, which Lanyon based on the medieval great halls of the Oxbridge universities. Also check out the **Naughton Gallery** (tel: 028-9097 3580; www.naughtongallery.org; Tue–Sun 11am–4pm) in the Lanyon Building, which houses the university's own art collection and

Exhibit at the Ulster Museum.

often hosts touring exhibitions. The **Brian Friel Theatre** (tel: 028-9097 1382; www.brianfrieltheatre.co.uk), named in honour of one of Ireland's most illustrious playwrights, is located on University Square.

Opposite the university's lawns is the modern Students' Union, which includes one of Belfast's best-known live music venues, **Mandela Hall** (tel: 028-9097 3726; www.mandelahall.com). There is also Elmwood Hall, a former Presbyterian church, above whose three-tiered spire a gilt weathercock catches the sun. At No. 28 is the Catholic Chaplaincy where the poet Philip Larkin (1922–85) wrote many of his finest lines during his five years working as a librarian at Queen's University. Back on University Road, past Methodist College on the right, the road divides into Malone and Stranmillis, the former a middle-class expanse of leafy avenues.

Just beyond the college, at No. 29 Malone Road, the **Ulster Historical Foundation** ❻ (tel: 028-9066 1988; www.ancestryireland.com) offers genealogical research for those on an ancestral quest.

ULSTER MUSEUM

Our route now enters the gates of the Botanic Gardens by the 1912 **statue to Lord Kelvin**, formulator of the Second Law of Thermodynamics.

Through the fir trees is the splendid **Ulster Museum** ❼ (tel: 0845 608 0000; www.nmni.com; Tue–Sun 10am–5pm; free). The museum features a 75ft (23m)-high glass-and-steel atrium, known as 'Window on Our World', that directs you to the history, art and nature zones. In the spectacular rooftop gallery the glass, jewellery and Belleek collections are shown off to their very best.

Adjacent to the museum is the ancient and beautiful **Friar's Bush** walled graveyard – this is Belfast's oldest Christian site, enshrouded by a sense

Making discoveries

With engaging displays, hands-on areas and a range of interactive programmes, a visit to the newly rejuvenated Ulster Museum will provide kids with a stimulating learning experience. There are all sorts of cool things for kids to discover: how big were dinosaurs? Want to see real treasure that was lost at sea? Well now you can find out. The explorer map and stickers are free of charge, available from the welcome area.

Everyone is an artist at the Ulster Museum.

The splendid Botanic Gardens and Palm House.

of ancient mystery. The site of the medieval friary of St Patrick, the graveyard contains the mysterious Friar's Stone with the date AD485 inscribed on it.

BOTANIC GARDENS

South of the Ulster Museum, Stranmills Gardens leads back into the **Botanic Gardens** ❽ (tel: 028-9031 4762; 7.30am–dusk; free) where a northwestern course through roses and hedged walks sets fair for both the Tropical Ravine and the **Palm House** (Apr–Sept Mon–Fri 10am–noon, 1–5pm, Sat–Sun 1–5pm, Oct–Mar until 3.45pm; free). In the ravine, created in 1889, water drips from banana leaves in a miniature sunken rainforest while palm fronds form exotic patterns against the glass dome of the Palm House, executed 50 years earlier by iron-founder Richard Turner (before he built the Great Palm House at Kew Gardens), to Lanyon's designs. The gardens are a regular venue for concerts and events including Belfast's annual Indian festival, Mela (www.belfastmela.org.uk). There is also a children's playground for the little ones to let off some steam.

Beyond the Palm House the north gate leads on to College Park and Botanic Avenue, while an optional diversion via the east gate takes you first through a district of neat red-brick terraces and a profligacy of churches, known as the Holy Land because so many of its street names derive from biblical cities. Local poet Padraic Fiacc lived in these streets and his poems are rooted here.

Ahead, on Botanic Avenue, is the formidable Scrabo stone mass of the **Union Theological College** ❾, with a colonnaded facade by Lanyon. Persuasive charm may gain you entry to the impressive – also colonnaded – domed library, used by Northern Ireland's House of Commons while it awaited Stormont's completion. Its Senate sat in the chapel.

BOTANIC AVENUE

The houses of Botanic Avenue retain, on their second and third floors, evidence of their 1870s origins. Deemed Belfast's Boul' Mich' (Boulevard St Michel in Paris) by Nobel Prize-winning poet Seamus Heaney, it now carries itself with a raffish louche air, its tree-lined pavements fronting on to bookmakers, bookshops and brasseries, B&Bs and coffee bars.

Well worth checking out here are Café Renoir at No. 95 for coffee and cake; at No. 50 the stylish Maggie May café (tel: 028-9032 2662; http://maggiemaysbelfastcafe.co.uk); at No. 83 the crime-specialist bookshop, No Alibis (tel: 028-90319061) with literary readings, live gigs and children's story time every Saturday morning; at No. 85 the jovial Italian restaurant Scalini (see box) and at Nos 59–63 Madison's Hotel (tel: 028-9050 9800; www.madisonshotel.com), with its eye-catching facade.

The atmospheric **Empire Music Hall** ⑩ (tel: 028-9024 9276; www.thebelfastempire.com) – housed in a deconsecrated church – provides live music and stand-up comedy (in university term time) as well as a lively bar. Go past Kingham Mission Church now, and you will find yourself back at Shaftesbury Square where we began.

Eating Out

Buskers
44 University Road; tel: 028-9020 2290; http://buskers.moondanceni.co.uk; Tue–Thu noon–9pm, Fri–Sat until 10pm, Sun until 8pm.
A strong emphasis on music is designed to enhance the diner's experience. Live music is held on Saturday nights, with traditional Irish music during the week. The superb home cooking draws the customers with favourites such as Portavogie scampi and chips or crab-claw linguini with chilli. ££

Deanes at Queens
1 College Gardens; tel: 028-9038 2111; www.michaeldeane.co.uk; Mon–Sat noon–3pm, 5.30–10pm, Sun 1–4pm.
Deanes brings contemporary sophistication to Queen's and a continental style of eating using simple local food prepared to perfection. The lunch menu is excellent value. An alfresco eating area overlooks the leafy College Gardens. ££

La Bastille
180a Lisburn Road; tel: 028-9066 7500; www.labastillerestaurant.com; daily noon–3pm, also Mon–Thu 5–10pm, Fri–Sat 5–11pm and Sun 5–9pm.
This chic restaurant has introduced refined French flavours to trendy Lisburn Road. Mussels in white wine, lemon sole and braised beef brisket with mashed potatoes are typical dishes. The menu du jour, with either two or three courses, is excellent value. It's worth the detour out of town for a special occasion. £££

Scalini
85 Botanic Avenue; tel: 028-9032 0303; www.scalinirestaurant.co.uk; Mon–Tue 5–10pm, Wed–Fri 5–11pm, Sat 4–11pm, Sun 4–9.30pm.
A Tuscan-inspired *trattoria* that gives the impression of being in Italy, where the extensive menu covers most Italian classics as well as dishes with a hint of Northern Ireland. ££

Tony Roma's
25–7 University Road; tel: 028-9032 6777; www.tonyromasbelfast.com; Mon–Thu 5–10pm, Fri 4–10.30pm, Sat 3–10.30pm, Sun 12.30–11pm.
Roma's has been throwing their famous baby back ribs on the grill for over 30 years and they are still just as good. Steak and seafood are always on the menu with the shrimp and salmon piccatta a big hit. ££

Town Square
45 Botanic Ave; tel: 079-38 244 851; http://townsquarebelfast.com; Mon–Thu 7am–10pm, Fri 7am–11pm, Sat 8am–11pm, Sun 8am–10pm.
Town Square café is part of the Crescent Townhouse. A simple menu featuring classics such as BBQ pulled-pork sandwiches and battered cod with mushy peas is perfectly complemented by the convivial, relaxed atmosphere. The adjoining Gin Bar serves cocktails, craft beer and ten types of gin. ££

The *Speaker* statue.

Tour 5

City Meets the Waterfront

This 2.5-mile (4km) half-day stroll revolves around the waterfront from Lanyon Place to Clarendon Dock and the streets behind to discover Belfast's seafaring history.

Belfast has a long maritime history that has become an integral part of the city's growing tourist industry. Following years of neglect, the Laganside Corporation was set up in 1989, and by attracting large levels of investment into the waterfront, successfully transformed the area. A smart promenade provides easy access, and development has subsequently spread to the docks area. Our tour also takes you behind the waterfront to see statues, monuments and other memorabilia, mostly associated with Belfast's watery past.

Highlights

- St George's Market
- Waterfront Hall
- Albert Memorial Clock
- Custom House
- Big Fish
- Sinclair Seamen's Presbyterian Church

AROUND CITY HALL

It may seem a little strange to begin this waterfront-themed walk at **City Hall** (see page 28), but it is here in the hall's grounds that you'll find the **Titanic Memorial** ❶. The *Titanic* was built in Belfast, and the connection is further honoured with the Belfast Titanic Maritime Festival, held every May in a celebration of the ship, her city and the artisan skills of the people who created her (see page 68).

At its base, two weeping sea-nymphs break the sea's cold grasp at

Spoilt for choice at St George's Market.

the feet of a scantily clad marble statue of a female Fame, in their arms the *Titanic*'s Unknown Soldier, an anonymous drowned man. An inscription in gold leaf records the names of 11 'gallant Belfast men who lost their lives on 15 April 1912 by the foundering of the Belfast-built *Titanic* through collision with an iceberg, on her maiden voyage from Southampton to New York'. But there is no mention of the dozens of doomed Belfast-born artisan crew and steerage-class passengers – or indeed of any women – on board. The 11 gallant men comprised the shipyard's Guarantee Group, which was checking performance targets on the vessel's maiden voyage. In 2012, a granite memorial listing the names of everyone who died in the tragedy was unveiled in a new *Titanic* Memorial Garden.

The Titanic Memorial in the grounds of City Hall.

Nearby, an aggressive bronze figure in a pith helmet and puttees serves as an 1899–1902 **Boer War cenotaph**. The rock on which he stands is, as was the custom of the times, supported by two bare-breasted and two flimsily covered goddesses.

Opposite, at Nos 11–13 Donegall Square East, is a hexastyle Corinthian porticoed facade, all that remains of the original once-grand 1840s Methodist church. Its congregation long

Secret marriage

May Street is named after the May family, who married Anna, an illegitimate daughter, to the second marquis of Donegall. Although they became sovereigns of the city, the snobbish marquis kept the marriage a secret.

gone to the suburbs, its 1,500-seat auditorium transferred from God to Mammon and its fine box pews cannibalised for pubs and restaurants, it has been rebuilt as the Ulster Bank's corporate headquarters. Harry Ferguson designed the minimal-maintenance Ferguson tractor, revolutionising British farming, at Nos 14–16. Other 19th-century shipbuilders lived at Nos 18–20. From Donegall Square East, we now head east down May Street to the waterfront.

MAY STREET

A great linen warehouse by Lanyon once stood at the top of May Street on the right, and another Lanyon creation, originally the Church of Ireland Diocesan offices, in polychrome brick, still stands opposite.

The provocative Reverend Henry Cooke preached in May Street's 1859 classically designed **Presbyterian Church ❷**. It was, after all, built as a vehicle large enough to accommodate both his ego and his 1,700-strong congregation. Nevertheless, he refused Temperance meetings and gave serious consideration to a proposal to use its basement cemetery as a bonded whiskey warehouse. These days the basement has been turned into the not-for-profit Urban Soul Café (Mon–Fri 9am–3pm; tel: 028-9032 5554) serving up soup, sandwiches, bagels, paninis and potato cakes. After you have feasted you can take a 30-minute tour of the church with a guide who will show you the impressive twin staircases, box pews, a mahogany gallery and fine timber-coffered ceiling.

To its east, towards the river, are the Doric columns of the church school. Almost opposite, Victoria Hall stands on the site of the Victoria Music Hall (built for amateur musicians) where, in 1882, a cornice fell, narrowly missing the novelist Charles Dickens while he was delivering a reading.

Auctioneers Ross & Co occupy the souk-like caverns of Nos 22–6, built in attractive brick and sandstone as the Presbyterian General Assembly's Office in 1875. Veterinary surgeon John Boyd Dunlop invented the first

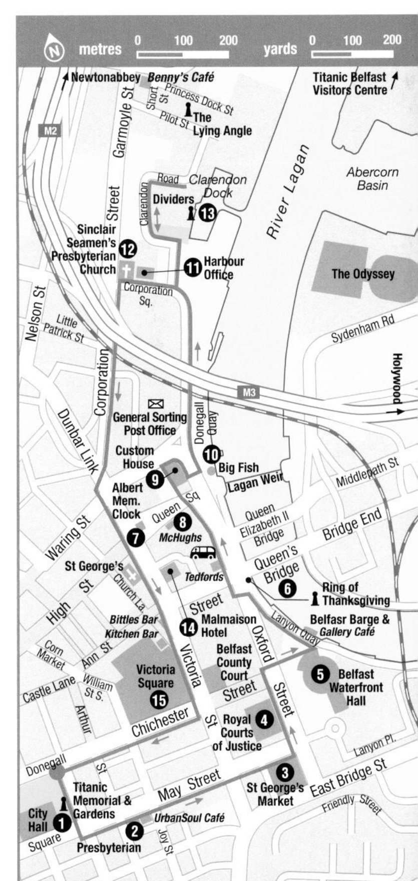

successful pneumatic tyre at Nos 38–42 and ran a hospital for sick horses where Telephone House now stands.

ST GEORGE'S MARKET

Beyond, on the corner with Verner Street, behind green faïence tiles, stands Ronnie Drew's (formerly called Magennis's Whiskey Café). Renamed after one of the mainstays of the famous Dubliners folk band, this attractive bar is now, unfortunately, infamous as the location of the murder of Robert McCartney in 2005. The brick, stone and iron Market House (1890), sympathetically restored to the original designs at a cost of more than £4 million, as **St George's Market** ❸ (tel: 028-9043 5704; www.belfastcity.gov.uk/stgeorgesmarket; Fri–Sun 8am–3pm) is all that is left of many such markets that peppered the Laganside end of May Street, in an area still known colloquially as The Markets.

The reopening in 1999 of St George's, the oldest covered market in Ireland, coincided with the movement towards farmers' markets and natural produce, so successfully harnessed at London's Borough Market. With a much smaller base of such suppliers, it has been hard for St George's to rival that level of excellence. However, after a sluggish start, it has really got into its stride. St George's Market sells a mix of everything; Saturday is the best day to find organically grown produce at the farmers' market as well as homemade cakes and bread.

Home-made scones for sale at St George's Market.

St George's also stages various special events and celebrations throughout the year, including craft fairs, the

St George's Market

St George's City Food, Craft and Garden Market (Sat 8am–3pm, Sun 10am–4pm) has become a genuine draw for foodies with all kinds of (mainly Irish) produce, from the best selection of Irish cheeses in Belfast to a wide range of freshly caught fish and seafood, organic meats and speciality breads, as well as flower stalls. The Variety Market (Fri 6am–2pm) sells books, antiques, second-hand clothes, fruit and vegetables, seafood and fish.

Local organic vegetables are a popular buy.

Night falls over Belfast Waterfront Hall.

Indian Festival of Colours, children's art workshops and Christmas markets. The Twilight Market is a periodic midweek event with pop-up restaurants, live music, food tastings, talks and demonstrations up until 11pm.

Royal Courts of Justice

Across May Street, west through iron security gates at the bottom of Chichester Street, stands the imposing neoclassical bulk of the **Royal Courts of Justice** ❹. Bewigged barristers and pinstriped solicitors parade, clutching pink-ribboned legal bundles, while miscreants, plaintiffs and their accusers and pursuers seem (mostly) in awe of the travertine marble vastness of the echoing central hall. Opposite is the Old Town Hall, completed in 1870, and now, after much bomb damage, restored as the **Belfast County Court**.

ON THE WATERFRONT

Opposite, in what is now Lanyon Place, where noisy, vibrant markets once thrived, dealing in cattle, flax, fruit, grain, horse, pork, potato, fish and all kinds of other goods, are the spare, sandy-coloured towers of the Hilton Hotel, a car park and the British Telecom building.

The towering buildings of Lanyon Place (see page 60) almost dwarf the stylishly emblematic **Belfast Waterfront Hall** ❺ (tel: 028-9033 4455; www.waterfront.co.uk) whose copper dome is as much a part of the Belfast skyline as the shipyard cranes, Samson and Goliath.

Take an evening stroll down by the Waterfront.

Belfast's most prestigious concert venue after the nearby Odyssey Arena, it regularly draws major rock and pop acts and is also worth checking out for drama, ballet, opera and musicals. Cross to the waterfront and head downstream, north towards **Queen's Bridge** ❻. Designed by Charles Lanyon and named after Queen Victoria, the bridge was built of Newry granite to replace the old Long Bridge, which had been *the* place in 1790 for an evening's *paseo*.

At the corner of Queen's Bridge, in what is now called Thanksgiving Square, visitors can enjoy the *Ring of Thanksgiving*. Created by Scottish artist Andy Scott, the 64ft (19.5m) stainless steel and bronze statue depicts a girl standing on a globe of the world, representing hope, aspiration and spirituality. Beyond Ann Street, along Donegall Quay, is **Tedfords** (tel: 028-9043 4000; www.tedfordsrestaurant.com), a quality bistro that was once a ship's chandler.

QUEEN'S SQUARE

Pass the Laganside Bus Centre and just beyond 'The Boat' apartment complex, glance left to see one of the city's most appealing vistas, **Queen's Square**. Until the 1840s, ships were tied up here at quays named after the Donegall family.

The restored McHughs Bar dates back to 1711.

On the square stands what was once Ireland's answer to Pisa's leaning tower, topped by the Gothic **Albert Memorial Clock** ❼.

The 113ft (34m) column is named after Queen Victoria's stern consort, who is displayed in his Garter robes. Lanyon secretly joined the committee that chose its design, but a decision to award him the contract was declared improper and the work went to his rival Barre.

Waterfront art

Exploration of Lanyon Place will uncover several interesting pieces of art and sculpture. Notable are Andy Scott's **Beacon of Hope** (2007) on Thanksgiving Square; Rita Duffy's **Dreams** (2004) on the Lanyon Quay building; **Barrel Man** (1997) by Ross Wilson on Café Terrace; and **Sheep on the Road** (1991) by Deborah Brown. The Welcome Centre has leaflets detailing the 30-plus pieces dotted around the Waterfront area, largely by artists with strong Belfast connections.

Watch out for *Sheep on the Road* on Lanyon Place.

Costume in place for the Belfast City Carnival at Custom House Square.

Built over reclaimed land, where once boats sailed down the River Farset (which now runs underneath), it had developed a serious list to match that of its more illustrious Italian rival. However, a painstaking restoration in 2003 ensured a more solid base and gave it such a thorough cleaning that it looks as new as the day it was built.

McHughs Bar ❽ (see page 67), on the left, claims to be Belfast's oldest extant building. Once a raffish collection of bordello taverns (a history reflected in one or two cheeky new details), it included Madame Du Barry's, where painter Stanley Spencer supped while his brother Gilbert 'Professor' Spencer played cathouse piano in the 1940s. Artfully restored by architect Dawson Stelfox, who was also responsible for the Albert Clock, it is a curious but successful mixture of old and new, with good food and regular music.

Across the square is another of Lanyon's solid accomplishments in Portland stone, rich in Ionic and Doric columns. Built in 1852 for the Northern Bank, it is the First Trust Bank.

CUSTOM HOUSE SQUARE

Beyond, to the north, **Custom House Square** has been restored to become the most important public space in Belfast. What had once been the lively Belfast version of 'Speakers' Corner' is marked with a life-size bronze statue, *The Speaker*; the square's surrounding copper lights continue the theme with their nickname the 'Hecklers'.

The square also includes Belfast's oldest drinking fountain for horses, the Calder fountain, restored to its former glory. A water feature traces the course of the Farset River beneath and there is a play area for children too.

The purpose of the £4.5-million restoration was to create a public space for special events and, since its launch in 2005, it has successfully done just that. It has seen everything from strongman competitions, circuses and carnivals to outdoor theatre performances, as well

Shimmering reflections along the Riverside Walk.

as Belfast's first outdoor Christmas ice rink, Belsonic outdoor music festival and Bierfest, a German beer festival. It is popular with skateboarders and office workers on sunny days.

The magnificent Palladian simplicity of the **Custom House** ❾ itself is the very zenith of Lanyon's achievements. Its real delight is a pediment of Britannia, Mercury and Neptune flanked by a lion and unicorn, amid capstans and knots, executed by the great stonemason Thomas Fitzpatrick and seen best from the Lagan Lookout. The novelist Anthony Trollope (1815–82) worked in the Custom House as a post office official in the 1850s.

THE LAGAN

Now our attention turns back to the river. The now-defunct Laganside Corporation was set up by the state in 1989 with a mission to reclaim, revitalise and gentrify the Lagan's banks, an area on which for so long the city had turned its back. First of its conquests was the river itself, previously little more than a mephitic cesspit of human and industrial effluent, torpid and foul smelling, exposing its detritus-despoiled mud banks in springtide days, dangerous and threatening when its flash-flood storm drains proved less than adequate.

The scheme also maintained a satisfactory water level upstream with the construction of **Lagan Weir** (see box) which, at a cost of £14 million, was one of the largest civil engineering projects ever to be undertaken in Northern Ireland at the time. In the event of a high tide, the weir also acts as a tidal barrage and can be used to protect the city from flooding.

Cleaning up the Lagan

Due to the massive purification measures carried out by Laganside Corporation, involving the construction of Lagan Weir, recultivating tributaries, dredging the banks and the installation of an aeration system, the River Lagan is welcoming back increasing numbers of plopping grey mullet, homing Atlantic salmon and wild brown trout to its greatly improved waters. Looking out on the River Lagan today, it is hard to believe these waters were ever polluted.

The Salmon of Knowledge

The Salmon of Knowledge is a 32ft (10m) ceramic-skinned salmon, commissioned to celebrate the return of salmon to the cleaned-up River Lagan. Created in 1999 by local artist John Kindness, the 'skin' is decorated with a mosaic of texts relating to Belfast's history, from material from Tudor times to recent newspaper headlines, and contributions from Belfast school children. An 'Ulster Fry' meal is pictured too.

Belfast's history depicted in the Big Fish's ceramic scales.

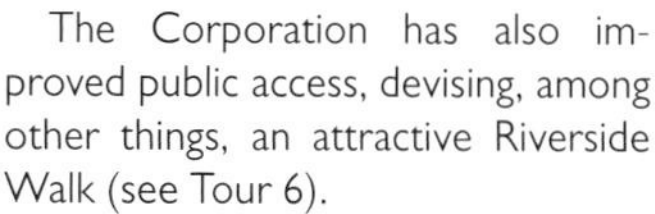

The Corporation has also improved public access, devising, among other things, an attractive Riverside Walk (see Tour 6).

Today, new and refurbished buildings overlook the river, making this one of the prime property locations in Belfast.

Donegall Quay

Just downstream of the weir is the pedestrianised **Donegall Quay**, with its massive river wall, bordered on one side with jetties and slipways; on the other, by practical but ornamental stone paviours and square-setts pierced by black bollards bearing the gilt seahorse from the city's coat of arms. Near here, in a city that is distinctive for the human scale of its buildings, is Northern Ireland's tallest building, the 26-storey office block Obel (standing for 'an obelisk set in old Belfast').

From here, by the **Big Fish** ⑩ sculpture (aka the *Salmon of Knowledge*), which celebrates the return of fish to the Lagan (see boxes), the Lagan Boat Company offers regular *Titanic* boat tours (tel: 028-9033 0844; www.laganboatcompany.com). On the tours, you can see the drawing rooms where the *Titanic* was designed, the dry dock where she was completed, the steam cranes that lowered her down and the slip streams from which she was launched, and get a commentary from genuine enthusiasts. The company also runs a number of special and seasonal tours throughout the year.

Belfast Harbour Office Clock.

The gigantic Harland & Wolff cranes dominate the skyline.

THE DOCKS

North along Donegall Quay, past the former ferry terminal, is Corporation Square with an elegant sandstone **Harbour Office ⓫**, an Italianate building decked out by Lanyon's partner, W.H. Lynn. Its boardroom features the captain's table and chairs that were destined for the *Titanic* but completed too late for the voyage, and is rich in fine historical paintings, including one of Captain Pirrie, grandfather to William, whose expansionist vision gave birth to the doomed liner. These riches can be inspected on request (tel: 028-9055 4422).

Just to the west of this is the late-1850s Italianate **Sinclair Seamen's Presbyterian Church ⓬**, designed by Lanyon. Its interior owes more, however, to an optimist and imbiber, the Reverend Sam Cochrane RN. The pitch-pine pulpit takes the shape of a ship's prow flanked by navigation lights. The font is a ship's binnacle. The bell of HMS *Hood* calls lost souls to service and collection boxes take the form of lifeboats. By the door

The bronze sculpture, *Dividers*, at Clarendon Dock.

The Belfast Barge

Moored at Lanyon Quay on the River Lagan, the Belfast Barge (028-9023 2555; Tue–Sat 10am–4pm) is home to the Maritime Museum, telling the industrial history of Belfast. Every second Saturday the Barge puts together a day of family programmes with different maritime themes. These include twice-daily storytelling, kids' crafts and activities as well as a child-friendly tour of the museum.

The stylish Malmaison hotel, a converted seed warehouse.

a text reads: 'A Merry Heart Doeth Good Like a Medicine'.

It is still the traditional duty of each incumbent minister to visit every ship that docks in Belfast Harbour. The church is open to the public on Wednesday afternoon, 2–4pm, and is well worth a visit.

Clarendon Dock

North of the Harbour Office, Clarendon Road leads into the redeveloped and attractive tree-lined riverside plazas surrounding **Clarendon Dock** ⓭. The trees are ash and oak, the boulevards laid with stone paviours and square-setts, like those on Donegall Quay, and many of the laid-up anchors and half-buried cannon bollards are authentic. Unable to pass unnoticed, the Vivien Burnside bronze sculpture, *Dividers*, represents an archway, as the viewer looks inwards to the changing city or outwards to the sea.

Across the River Lagan looms the huge yellow upturned 'U's of the cranes, called Samson and Goliath, and The Odyssey (see Tour 9).

> **Sailortown**
>
> North of Clarendon Dock was a once thriving dockland community known as Sailortown, and since 2009 it has undergone redevelopment. New housing has changed the character of the area but it retains a whiff of its old atmosphere. To experience a true Belfast caff, stop off at Benny's Café in Short Street (Mon–Fri 7am–4pm, Sat until 2pm) and tuck into Benny's Belfast Bap.

VICTORIA STREET

Turning back, through Clarendon Dock and then west along Corporation Square and under the motorway, we eventually join Victoria Street and continue until we reach High Street. While the Chapel of the Ford stood on the corner of High Street from at least 1306, its ultimate successor, the high Anglican **St George's**, dates only from 1813. Its classical portico was brought from the Earl Bishop of Derry's unfinished house. Perks for its first choir boys included all the salmon they could catch from the River Farset beyond the original wrought-iron rear gates. A plain memorial to Henry Pottinger is in tune with its plain interior.

Carry on along Victoria Street to the **Malmaison hotel** ⓮ (see page 125) with its curious frontage. The building is decorated with Thomas Fitzpatrick's splendid stonework, first devised for Lytle's and McCausland's Warehouses (rival seed merchants), Nos 34–8 Victoria Street. For Lytle he carved frogs between water lilies, squirrels eating nuts, plus an assortment of exotic birds. For McCausland he represented the five trading continents in five robustly non-PC heads: Africa – an Ethiopian slave with broken chain and Nile lily; Asia – a Chinese girl in silks; Oceania – a South Sea Islander with coconuts; Europe – a

Inside Victoria Square shopping centre complex.

be-whiskered and self-satisfied Caucasian; North America – an indigenous 'Indian' complete with tomahawk and feather headdress.

Bittles Bar (see page 67), probably the world's only triangular pub, is tucked into the gridiron-shaped building at the corner of Victoria Street and Upper Church Lane. The bar was once known as the Shakespeare and was patronised by performers from nearby theatres.

Victoria Square

Just across the street, the venerable **Kitchen Bar** (see page 67) has settled in well to its new accommodation, having been forced out of its nearby 1859-built premises by the construction of the mammoth **Victoria Square** ⓯ (028-9032 2277; www.victoriasqaure.com) retail development just next door. Belfast's newest and largest shopping and leisure complex, built at a cost of £320 million, occupies four floors and is topped by a massive glass dome construction. The dome houses a viewing gallery and is the perfect place to grasp the dimensions of the cityscape and surrounding hills.

Standing at the entrance to the shopping centre is an eye-catching Victorian fountain. Made in 1874 by George Smith & Company in Glasgow, the ornate **Jaffe Fountain** was first sited in Victoria Square before being moved to the Botanic Gardens, but has now been returned to its original location where the many thousands of shoppers every day will be able to appreciate it. It is dedicated to Daniel Joseph Jaffe (1809–74) who was born in Mecklenburg, Germany and was responsible for laying the foundation stone of the synagogue in Great Victoria Street.

Jaffe is buried in the Jewish plot at Belfast Cemetery. Daniel Joseph's son, Otto Jaffe, was elected as Belfast's first lord mayor in 1899, knighted after his first term and re-elected as lord mayor in 1904.

CHICHESTER STREET

Back on Victoria Street once more, carry on and then take the first right into Chichester (which local people pronounce Chai-Chester) Street; look eastwards for a splendid vista of the Waterfront Hall, then west to the Black Mountain. The pleasant Garrick Bar at No. 29, built in 1810, took its name from the famous English actor; its current customers ply other stages – although they may be just as dramatic – the nearby Petty Sessions and Royal Courts of Justice.

Just to the west, Nos 7–11 form an excellently restored terrace of four-storey Georgian houses built in dusky brick and dating from 1804. They almost complete this route, which now proceeds across Donegall Square East from the red sandstone of the Ocean Buildings, rich in exotic carvings of mermaids and monsters.

To finish as we started, right in the corner of the City Hall grounds, there stands – with ship's plans at hand – yet another reminder of the *Titanic*: a Sicilian marble statue of Sir Edward James Harland of Harland & Wolff, the shipbuilding company.

Eating Out

Bittles Bar
70 Upper Church Lane; tel: 028-9031 1088; Mon–Sat 11am–11.30pm, Sun until 6pm.
Bright oil murals depicting the Troubles and gilded shamrocks bring this beautiful old pub to life. It's very popular with shoppers who drop by here for a much-needed respite and refreshments at reasonable prices. £

Holohans at the Barge
1 Lanyon Quay; tel: 028-9023 5973; www.holohansatthebarge.co.uk; Tue–Thu 5–11pm, Fri–Sat until midnight (last dinner orders 9.30pm), Sun 1–4pm.
This restaurant is the ideal place for a romantic meal on a Barge, moored behind the Waterfront Hall, and is an idyllic spot from which to survey the river traffic. The menu features seafood favourites such as seared scallops and local specialities such as boxty. ££

Kitchen Bar
1 Victoria Square; tel: 028-9024 5268; www.thekitchenbar.com; Mon–Wed 11.30am–11pm, Thu 11.30am–midnight, Fri–Sat noon–1am, Sun noon–9pm.
Relocated from its original site around the corner to accommodate the Victoria Square development, nothing else has changed at the Kitchen Bar – it's still full of charm, still friendly and still renowned for its quality, home-cooked traditional food. Famous for the Paddy Pizza (soda bread, scallions, Irish ham, local cheese and tomato). £

Malmaison Brasserie
34–8 Victoria Street; tel: 028-9022 0200; www.malmaison.com; Mon–Fri 7–10am, noon–2.30pm, 6–10.30pm, Sat 8–11am, noon–2.30pm, 6–10.30pm, Sun 8–11am, 12.30–4.30pm, 6–10pm.
Elegant booths and comfy armchairs provide the perfect blend of sumptuous surroundings and an informal atmosphere. The menu of locally sourced food lets you sample uncomplicated French-style cuisine prepared with care and passion. Rumour has it they do the best *crème brûlée* in Belfast. £££

McHughs Bar and Restaurant
29–31 Queen's Square; tel: 028-9050 9999; www.mchughsbar.com; restaurant Mon–Sat 5–10pm, Sun noon–9pm; bar food Mon–Sat noon–7pm.
This traditional pub with a difference has a 100-seater restaurant where many of its original features dating from 1711 are retained. Pub grub is traditional Belfast pub classics such as boxty and baked gammon. The restaurant fare is more sophisticated, with steamed Dundrum mussels and slow-roasted local ham hock on offer. £–££

Tedfords
5 Donegall Quay; tel: 028-9043 4000; www.tedfordsrestaurant.com; Thu–Fri noon–2.30pm, Tue–Sat 5–9.30pm.
In keeping with its maritime traditions, freshly caught fish features on the menu, although the succulent steaks are popular, too. Tedfords overlooks the waterfront and attracts many loyal locals. ££–£££

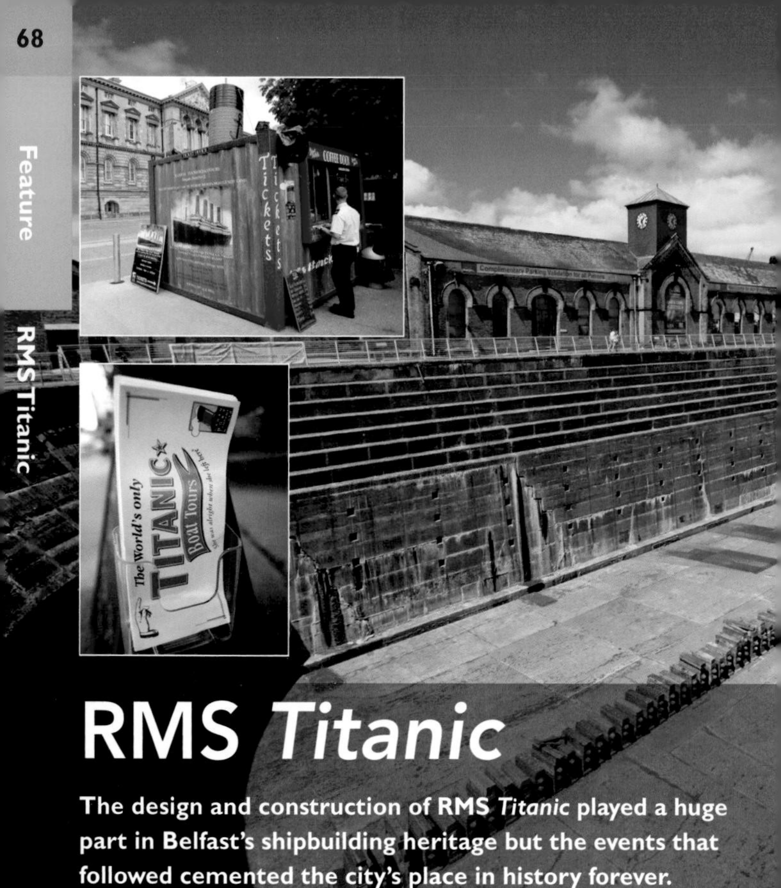

RMS *Titanic*

The design and construction of RMS *Titanic* played a huge part in Belfast's shipbuilding heritage but the events that followed cemented the city's place in history forever.

Despite its sad watery fate in 1912, *Titanic* was a remarkable feat of Edwardian engineering – innovative, superbly crafted and built on an extraordinary scale. It was, in other words, an appropriate and easily identifiable symbol of Belfast's pre-eminence as a shipbuilder. By the time City Hall was built in 1906, the city was not only one of the world's greatest ports but also a world leader in rope making, tobacco and other industries. *Titanic* was thus built at the apex of Belfast's ambition, belief and sense of self-importance. Designed and built in the city between 1909 and 1912 and waved off on her maiden voyage on 2 April 1912, she was the most luxuriously appointed ship ever seen, the pride and joy of shipbuilders Harland and Wolff.

THE TITANIC BOOM

More than 100 years on, there are those among the more sceptical local people who question the wisdom of Belfast identifying itself ever more closely with a ship famous for sinking on its maiden voyage. Such voices of dissent carry little weight these days – this city is very proud of its associations with the greatest liner ever built and for the centennial commemorations in 2012 it unveiled

Titanic's dry dock and pumphouse.

Titanic snippets

It cost $7,500,000 to build the *Titanic.*
The launch took 62 seconds to complete.
There were 29 boilers on board and her forward anchor weighed nearly 16 tons.
More than 3 million rivets were used in the building of the ship.
She was 882ft (268m) long and weighed 46,328 tons fully loaded.
She had 5 miles (8km) of decks, squash courts, and was the first vessel to have a heated swimming pool.
First-class passengers paid a whopping $4,350 for a parlour suite ticket.
Titanic hit an iceberg on Sunday 14 April 1912 at about 11.40pm and sank at 2.20am on 15 April.
The ship was loaded with only enough lifeboats for 1,178 people; there were 2,228 people on board.
The largest percentage of survivors were first-class passengers.
The *Titanic* lies 12,460ft (3,798m) down at the bottom of the Atlantic.
Of the 1,517 people who perished, only 306 bodies were recovered.

the spectacular Titanic Belfast Visitor Centre. A major annual festival called 'Belfast's Titanic Maritime Festival' is also firmly established on the city's calendar of events every May. The Titanic Quarter, a £1-billion mini-city of apartments, hotels, restaurants, bars and visitor attractions on 185 acres (75 hectares) of the former shipyard where the legendary liner was born, is dedicated to this amazing ship (see page 84).

TOURS

Throughout the streets of Belfast there are numerous buildings and monuments with links to the *Titanic.* A myriad of guided tours provide an insight into the remarkable history of Belfast's greatest attraction. The best starting point for a self-guided tour is the Titanic Belfast Visitor Centre. For more information about *Titanic* visit the website of the Belfast Titanic Society at www.belfast-titanic.com.

Tour 6

Riverside Walk

A circular stroll of 3.5 miles (5.5km), along the banks of the River Lagan from the centre of Belfast, with the option of a longer towpath bike ride.

This tour follows the riverside walkway both sides of the riverbank, pausing in Ormeau Park. Alternatively, you can hire a bike and explore the Lagan Towpath, a total of 11 miles (18km), taking you all the way to Lisburn.

Highlights

- Waterfront Hall
- Ormeau Park
- Cycling the Lagan towpath
- Lagan Meadows
- Barnett's Demesne

STARTING THE WALK

Starting at **Waterfront Hall** ❶ the river walkway heads south along the left bank to May's Meadow, where it crosses Albert Bridge to St George's Harbour and continues past the business park. Continue to **Ormeau Bridge**; cross the bridge and take the first gates into **Ormeau Park** ❷ (7.30am–dusk), which features some unusual trees, eco-trails and orienteering courses, and has two children's playgrounds.

The bridges

Leave the park on the east side onto Ravenhill Road and continue to **Albert Bridge**. Cross the road and rejoin the towpath, continuing to Laganview, Gregg's Quay and under Queen's Bridge. At the next bridge, Queen Elizabeth II Bridge, go under the main road, pick up the path again and continue to **Lagan Weir**, a good place to cross back to the west bank.

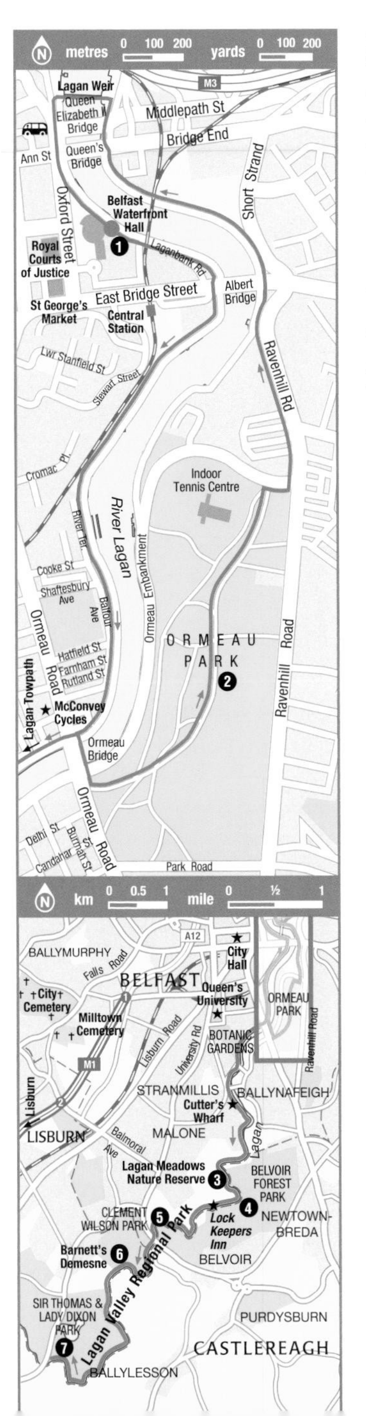

CYCLING THE TOWPATH

To hire a bike, consider signing up for the **Belfast Bike** scheme (www.belfastbikes.co.uk), with 40 docking locations dotted across the city. The first half-hour is free; the charge is only 50p per half-hour for the next 4 hours and £2 per half-hour afterwards.

Along the canal linen barons' mansions recall its role in a 19th-century plan to create a Belfast-to-Dublin water route. The path descends through grasslands into **Lagan Meadows Nature Reserve ❸**. Another footbridge across the Lagan leads into **Belvoir Forest Park ❹**. Otherwise follow the left bank downstream, crossing a wooded island between canal and river. Left-bank explorers can continue upstream by **Clement Wilson Park ❺**, and past **Shaw's Bridge**, where there's a possible diversion to **Barnett's Demesne ❻** with an elegant 1820s house, restaurant and art gallery. Another point of interest is **Sir Thomas and Lady Dixon Park ❼** with its mansion and magnificent rolling acres. The towpath continues on to Lisburn.

Eating Out

Cutter's Wharf Bar and Grill
Lockview Road, Stranmillis; tel: 028-9080 5100; www.cutterswharf.co.uk; daily noon–9pm.
Bistro-style menu and daily specials including posh fish and chips, steaks with thrice-cooked chips and meat-feast burgers. Dine outside in fine weather. £–££

Lock Keepers Inn
2 Lock Keepers Lane, Lagan towpath; tel: 028-9064 0088; Tue–Sun 8.30am–5pm.
Snacks, ranging from sandwiches to scones, sausage rolls and soups, are served at this idyllic location overlooking the River Lagan. £

Crumlin Road Courthouse.

Tour 7

Northern Suburbs

This 7-mile (11km) drive incorporates one of Belfast's most infamous stretches of road; afterwards, visit Belfast Castle then take the challenge of a 2-mile (4km) uphill walk.

Close to the city centre along the once troublesome Crumlin Road and in the Ardoyne district are some grim reminders of a turbulent past. It is hard to believe that the pleasant suburbs and Belfast Hills are so close at hand, where you can discover riches such as Belfast Castle and the zoo, and throw caution to the wind and climb high above the city. If you don't want to drive, take the direct route to the castle or the zoo on Metro bus 1 from the city centre, heading out along the Antrim Road.

CLIFTON STREET

From the city centre take Donegall Street, which leads into Clifton Street, and the junction of North Queen Street. Once known as the Poorhouse,

Highlights

- Clifton House
- Crumlin Road Gaol
- Belfast Castle
- Cave Hill
- Belfast Zoo

Clifton House ❶ (2 North Queen Street; tel: 028-9089 7534; http://cliftonbelfast.com), though much altered, is still one of the most delightfully modest public Georgian buildings in Ireland and one of Belfast's oldest. After lengthy restoration, the building is now a unique event venue and a Heritage Centre which runs guided tours every Friday at 3pm.

Virtually opposite, at 86 Clifton

Statue of King William III on top of Belfast Orange Hall on Clifton Street.

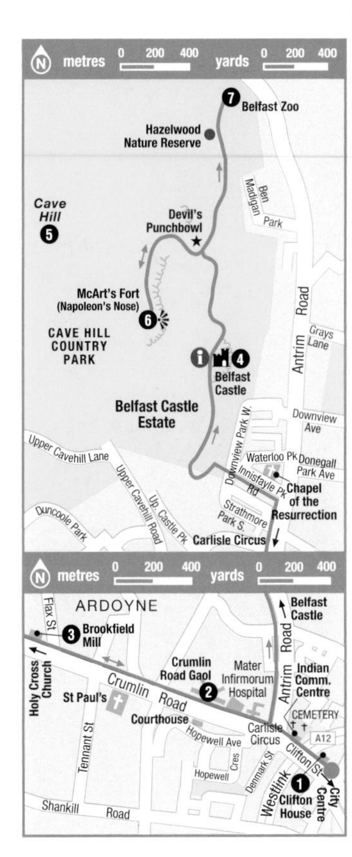

Street, is the **Indian Community Centre** (tel: 028-9024 9746; www.iccbelfast.com) housing a Hindu temple. It organises many events throughout the year, including the Mela festival in August, which brings thousands to Botanic Gardens for Indian dancing, music, fashion and food.

One of the most important burial sites in Belfast is the **Clifton Street Cemetery**, where a great number of pioneers of Belfast life lie, including politicians, journalists, Henry Joy McCracken and his sister Mary Ann, and the man who coined the phrase 'Emerald Isle', Dr William Drennan.

CRUMLIN ROAD GAOL

North past Carlisle Circus are Charles Lanyon's deliberately sinister **Crumlin Road Gaol** ❷ (tel: 028-9074 1500; www.crumlinroadgaol.com; daily 10am–4.30pm) and his formidable Corinthian **Courthouse**, facing each other across – and joined by a tunnel below – the Crumlin Road. During the worst years of the Troubles, between 1969 and 1996, the prison held some of the most notorious murderers, including many involved in paramilitary violence. After a £10m restoration it has been transformed to reflect the way it looked in Victorian times. A 75-minute tour takes in the holding, punishment and condemned cells.

Further on up the Crumlin Road is the beautifully converted **Brookfield Mill** ❸, once part of Belfast's linen industry. At the apex of Crumlin Road and nearby Woodvale, the peace line marks off Catholic Ardoyne, where some 20,000 people were employed in the linen mills. Look out for Ross Wilson's bronze statute, *The Mill Worker*, outside the building, inspired by the artist William Conor's depiction of the 'shawlies' (female mill workers).

Saving Cave Hill

The Cave Hill Conservation Campaign (www.cavehillconservation.org) is a voluntary group of around 100 people originally founded in 1989 to stop prospecting for minerals taking place in this place of outstanding natural beauty. Its remit has extended beyond this and the group is dedicated to preserving Cave Hill by reducing litter, planting trees and keeping rights of way open, as well as organising wildlife events. The area is well worth preserving; on a clear day you can see the hills of the Lake District on the UK mainland.

BELFAST HILLS

Returning to Carlisle Circus, turn north into the lengthy **Antrim Road**, and you will pass the pleasant Waterworks Park, which dates from an 1840s attempt to solve Belfast's growing water needs.

Looking west, north or east from almost anywhere in Belfast you can see how the city is cupped in a saucer of hills. Clockwise from the west, they are the Black Mountain, Cave Hill, the Castlereagh Hills and the drumlins of County Down, all framed at the ends of the shallow canyons of the streets.

Just over 1.5 miles (2km) on along Antrim Road is Innisfayle Park Road, which leads to Belfast Castle.

BELFAST CASTLE

Follow the road into the castle estate and up to **Belfast Castle** ❹ (tel: 028-9077 6925; www.belfastcastle.co.uk; Mon 9.30am–4pm, Tue–Thu until 7pm, Fri–Sat until 9pm, Sun 9am–4pm; free), a ruggedly romantic Scots baronial pile rich in turrets and faced with Cookstown sandstone. It was constructed in 1865 for the impoverished third marquis of Donegall, by Charles Lanyon's son, John, who borrowed freely from Prince Albert's sketches for Balmoral Castle. John Lanyon's fees were guaranteed by the marquis's daughter, Harriet, who had taken the sensible precaution of marrying the immensely rich eighth earl of Shaftesbury. Their son, the ninth earl, presented the castle to the city in 1934. Private tours of the castle are available on request. There is also the Cellar restaurant and an excellent adventure playground in the grounds (Apr–Sept daily, Oct–Mar Sat–Sun only). The drive continues back to the Antrim Road north towards Belfast Zoo.

The breathtaking view from Cave Hill.

The grounds of Belfast Castle with a cat mosaic.

The Cave Hill Visitor Centre at the castle has detailed walking maps and other information on the building's history as well as its natural surroundings in the Cave Hill Country Park.

CAVE HILL WALK

We now begin our **Cave Hill** ❺ walk proper through the 200-acre (80-hectare) estate. Take the Cave Hill Trail from the car park. From the woods a steeper path goes all the way to the **Devil's Punchbowl**, first used by Neolithic hunter-gatherers. Just before this cave the trail takes a left turn running steeply towards a defensive ditch to **McArt's Fort** ❻ on the 1,180ft (360m)-high promontory. This is alternatively referred to as **Napoleon's Nose** or Ben Madigan (from *beann*, the Irish for peak) after a 9th-century king of Ulster. The outline of Cave Hill has been likened to an outline of Napoleon sleeping on the hillside, the fort representing his nose. Here foxes trail rabbits through the heather and badgers wander at night through the bluebells in May.

Belfast Zoo

The Cave Trail continues to Hightown Fort, but if you wish to walk to the zoo return part way to the Devil's Punchbowl and take the path north, along to **Hazelwood Nature Reserve**. This path brings you to the perimeter of **Belfast Zoo** ❼ (tel: 028-9077 6277; www.belfastzoo.co.uk; Oct–Mar daily 10am–4pm, Apr–Sept until 7pm).

Built in the early 19th century as part of a pleasure ground at the end of the tram route, the zoo has a pleasantly old-fashioned feel, but, in fact, is remarkably progressive in its captive breeding programme for rare animals. The views from here are particularly splendid. Lemurs are allowed to stroll freely around the zoo; the African Enclosure and the penguin and sea lion pools are popular with children. The Adventurers' Learning Centre is the zoo's new play area. Call for further information on their unique 'Keeper for a Day' and 'Meet the Animals' programmes.

Eating Out

Cellar Restaurant

Belfast Castle, Antrim Road; tel: 028-9077 6925; www.belfastcastle.co.uk; Mon 9.30am–4pm, Tue–Sat until 9pm, Sun until 4.30pm.

An atmospheric place for breakfast or lunch, and a romantic setting for an evening meal. Local produce features extensively on the menu, including Ballycastle lamb and Portavogie mussels. ££

Treetop Tearoom

Belfast Zoo, Antrim Road; tel: 028-9077 6277; www.belfastzoo.co.uk; Apr–Sept daily 10am–5.30pm

This is a fairly basic café providing sandwiches and drinks, but it affords a spectacular view over Belfast Lough and the zoo. There is another café near the zoo's entrance called The Lion's Den Restaurant which serves hot meals. £

Mural in the Falls Road commemorating Bobby Sands.

Tour 8

West Belfast

This 2.5-mile (4km) half-day walk covers one of the most absorbing and controversial Belfast districts, now becoming the focus of a tourist boom.

West Belfast has witnessed some unthinkable things in its turbulent past and this tour gives the opportunity to learn and understand a bit of what life was like before, after and during the Troubles. Many famous landmarks from over three decades of the area's history are here. One of the most striking discoveries is just how closely situated the Shankill and Falls roads are, where two very different communities still live. The tour follows the length of both roads and enables you to cross the Peace Line.

Highlights

- Murals
- Clonard Monastery
- An Cultúrlann McAdam Ó Fiaich
- City Cemetery
- Peace Line
- St Matthew's Church

TAKING A TAXI

As an alternative to this walk, you might consider taking one of the famous **Black Taxi Tours** (try Big E's Belfast Taxi Tours; tel: 079-6847 7924; www.big-e-taxitours.com or The Belfast Black Taxi Tour; tel: 028-9064 2264; www.belfasttours.com). They give a detailed insight into the area, its people and what makes the district what it is today.

FALLS ROAD

For republican west Belfast start at the city centre end (take Metro bus

An environmental focus

Fáilte Feirste Thiar, the organisation behind the promotion of West Belfast Tourism, has joined with the West Belfast Partnership Board to work with the local community in improving the neighbourhood's environment and the health of its inhabitants. The Gruffalo Trail is now open at Colin Glen Forest Park with magical recreations of each character by sculptor Andrew McIntyre. More details of this family event can be found on www.visitwestbelfast.com.

10) of the **Falls Road**, at the junction with Northumberland Street. Though many high-rise tower blocks have been demolished, the Divis Tower, to the east, is still standing as a testament to the horrors of the Troubles. The British army set up an observation point on the top two floors, which could only be accessed by helicopter. This is where nine-year-old Patrick Rooney – the first child victim of the Troubles – was killed in 1969. Just off the Falls Road is **St Peter's Cathedral ❶** (St Peter's Square; tel: 028-9032 7573; www.stpeterscathedralbelfast.com; Mon–Sat 9am–4pm), whose two great towers with rising spires were used as sightlines by German bombers in World War II.

Conway Mill ❷ (5–7 Conway Street; tel: 028-9032 9646; www.conwaymill.org; Tue–Sat 9am–5pm), the second turning to the right up the Falls Road, was built in 1842 by the Kennedy family, and it was the first flax-spinning mill in west Belfast. A listed building, it ceased production in 1972 and is now a centre for more than 20 local craftspeople including artists and jewellery makers. It also houses the small **Irish Republican History Museum** which is entirely run by volunteers and displays a fascinating range of artefacts.

Bobby Sands Memorial

Back on the Falls Road, just two streets up on the right is Sevastapol Street, on the corner of which is the iconic memorial mural for Bobby Sands, elected MP as he lay dying, who was the first of the 10 republican hunger strikers to die, aged 27, after a 66-day fast in 1981. This mural is one of the most photographed pieces of public art in Europe.

Clonard Monastery

A little further on, at the end of Clonard Street, is **Clonard Monastery ❸** (tel: 028-9044 5950; www.clonard.com; Mon–Sat 9am–7pm, Sun until 2pm). Built in French Gothic style with a striking 20ft (6m)-wide stained-glass rose window, the impressive church and monastery were completed in 1911. You can trace the history of its owners, the Redemptorist order, a Catholic movement founded in Italy in 1732, on floor and ceiling mosaics. In early summer, the church hosts a nine-day Novena when the grounds are crowded with the faithful.

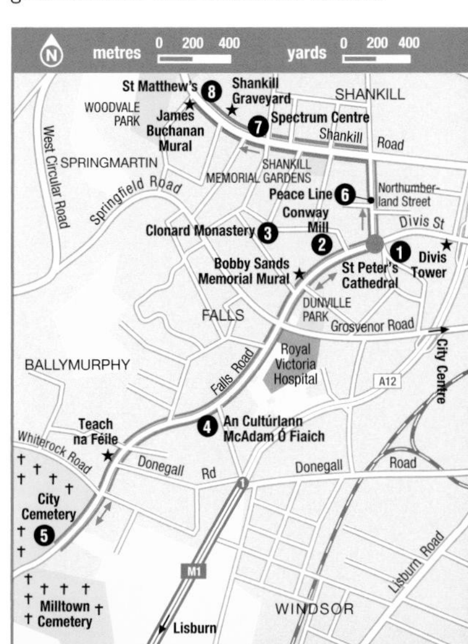

It is here that vital talks were held that ultimately led to the peace process. The church is also used as part of the West Belfast Festival (see page 79).

On the other side of the Falls Road, Dunville Park is named after its whiskey-distilling benefactor, who donated the park to the people of the city in 1887. Located within the park is the famous Dunville Fountain, which has been refurbished and is now filled with 6,000 flowers. Further up the road, the sprawling grounds of Royal Victoria Hospital still house the world's first air-conditioning ducts. Another regular venue for the West Belfast Festival is St Mary's University College to the right, designed in High Victorian style and dating from 1900.

Gaeltacht Quarter

This district is focused on the Falls Road. Continuing along the road and central to this area is **An Cultúrlann McAdam Ó Fiaich** ❹ (tel: 028-9096 4180; www.culturlann.ie), a three-storey Irish language, arts and cultural centre at No. 216. It has a café, Irish-language book and gift shop, theatre and tourist information point. On the ground floor, the Dillon Gallery, named after the Falls Road artist Gerard Dillon, who spent time painting in the west of Ireland, mounts shows by local and international artists. The gallery was opened in 2011 as part of a £2m renovation and extension to mark the centre's 20th anniversary. The building also houses the radio station Raidió Fáilte. Live traditional and contemporary music sessions, concerts and a children's art programme also feature. Stop here for a coffee and soak up the atmosphere while discovering the essence of Irish culture.

From here you can book authentic political walking tours of the area, organised by former republican prisoners. Coiste (10 Beechmount Avenue, off the Falls Road; tel: 028-9020 0770; www.coiste.ie), run tours that gather at Divis Tower in the Lower Falls (Tue, Thu, Sat, Sun 11am) and visit the murals of the Falls Road. It can be arranged to hand you over to former loyalist prisoners at the Peace Line for a tour of the Shankill Road. There are also tours focusing on the Milltown Cemetery, the Ballymurphy housing estate and the history of the United Irishmen. Tours are available in several European languages. Tickets can be purchased at the Belfast Welcome Centre (tel: 028-9024 6609) or through the Coiste website; booking is essential.

Clonard Monastery.

West Belfast Festival

The West Belfast (Féile An Phobail) Festival office is just up the road at Teach na Féile (No. 473; tel: 028-9031 3440; www.feilebelfast.com). The original festival has spawned several oth-

Celtic cross headstones at Milltown Cemetery.

ers including: the Draocht Children's Arts festival in October, the Laugh at the Bank comedy festival in May and the Traditional Spring Festival (Féile An Earraigh) in March. Usually held in early August, the West Belfast Festival – or Féile An Phobail, meaning 'festival of the people' – is a mixture of music, drama, literary events and comedy, with major names such as Roddy Doyle, Christy Moore and Stephen Rea participating. Highlights include heated political debates and a colourful parade up the Falls. It is now the biggest community-based festival in Ireland.

Founding the festival

The West Belfast Festival was founded in 1988 when the Falls Road district was described by the international media as a broken, crime-ridden community. The founders were determined to promote the positive side of the neighbourhood and it has gone from strength to strength, creating one of the best-attended festivals in the city, bringing in some 50,000 people. It's a great time to be in town.

The Cemeteries

Continuing up to the top end of the Falls Road you come to the cemeteries. Though it might seem perverse, one of the most fascinating tours in Belfast is during the festival when a local Sinn Féin councillor and former Belfast Lord Mayor, Tom Hartley, takes visitors on a 90-minute journey around the **City Cemetery** ❺ and **Milltown Cemetery**, the former owned by Belfast City Council, the latter by the Catholic Church. Milltown, where, on live TV, loyalist paramilitary Michael Stone shot and threw grenades at mourners at a republican funeral, includes the plot where hunger striker Bobby Sands is buried.

Despite the sunken wall that prevents Catholic and Protestant bodies from mingling underground, the real story of the City Cemetery is more complex. Here lie the great and good of Belfast, men who shaped the city. Yet, the most striking features of their tombs are the Celtic crosses and the

Painted walls on the Shankill Road.

seeming acceptance of a cultural Irishness that would have contrasted sharply with their political loyalties. By 1921 the effects of partition become apparent in an absence of Irish symbols and the frequency of Union flags. There are many fine monuments within the City Cemetery, some in excellent condition while others have been vandalised over the years. Both cemeteries can be visited during normal opening hours.

The Falls and Shankill

Though poverty and lack of resources still affect both communities, they seem far more pronounced in the Shankill, a heartland of loyalism. Redevelopment has not been sympathetic or universal; there are many empty sites and decaying buildings, and it is estimated that nearly half the population of the area has left over the past three decades. Compared to the more cohesive and vibrant republican community on the Falls, there is a noticeable listlessness and lack of bustle.

The tour goes back down the Falls Road; you may choose to walk, but we suggest taking either Metro bus 10 or buses 82/82A and disembarking at the corner with Northumberland Street.

PEACE LINE

Walk along Northumberland Street to the north and through the **Peace Line** ❻ towards the **Shankill Road**. On 9 September 1969, James Chichester-Clarke, prime minister of Northern Ireland's parliament, announced that the British army would build a temporary 'peace line' between Protestant and Catholic areas of Belfast to stop rioting. By the end of the century there were 15 walls separating the two communities, some of them corrugated-iron barriers crowned with razor wire, others 20ft (6m) concrete barricades reminiscent of the Berlin Wall. The most obtrusive stretched for 2 miles (3km), separating the Falls and Shankill roads. The walls have now become a tourist attraction, but some local people believe they are still needed. Stormont have committed to removing the peace walls by 2023.

SHANKILL ROAD

At the junction with the Shankill Road, turn west past the Rex Bar and the famous mural of Edward Carson signing the 1912 Covenant, and you will come to the Shankill Memorial Gardens, on the other side of the road. The gardens recall those who died in the two world wars, with an old Belfast street lamp with an 'eternal flame' commemorating the victims of the 1993 Shankill Road bombing.

Spectrum Centre

Although the presence of loyalist paramilitaries is still keenly felt, the £4.5 million **Spectrum Centre** ❼ (331–3 Shankill Road, tel: 028-9050 4555; www.spectrumcentre.com) opened in 2001, a rough equivalent of An Cultúrlann McAdam Ó Fiaich on the Falls, has become a base for community groups as well as dance, drama and music studios, sports venues and a film society. This is Shankill's answer to the Troubles, a community-based centre reaching out to a wider audience, giving confidence, creative expression and a positive approach for the future.

Churches and cemeteries

Towards the top of the road, on the right, is the Shankill Graveyard, the main city cemetery until 1866. It is said burials have taken place on this site for over 1,000 years. It contains the graves of several notable citizens as well as many who died in various plagues. A statue of Queen Victoria stands by the main entrance. The name Shankill comes from the Gaelic for 'Old Church', the site of which, believed to date from the 6th century, can be found within the graveyard.

Just up the road is the distinctive 1872 Church of Ireland **St Matthew's** ❽, known as the 'Shamrock Church', for its tri-cornered shape. Its holy water font is believed to be the only remnant in Belfast of the original Old Church (and whose water is also believed to be a cure for warts).

Nearby is another famous mural, depicting James Buchanan, one of several US presidents with Ulster antecedents. From here you can catch the Metro bus 11 back to the city centre.

Eating Out

Andrea's Milkshake Shop
272 Shankill Road; tel: 028-9032 9624; Mon–Fri and Sun noon–10pm, Sat 11am–10pm.
If you are looking for a milkshake, slushie, ice-cream or sweet treat, this is the place to come. £

Applejacks Coffee Shop
1 Caffrey Hill, Glen Road; tel 028-9043 1125; Mon–Fri 8am–4.30pm, Sat 9am–4.30pm, Sun noon–4pm.
Enjoy beautiful views from the outdoor terrace of this pretty family-run café. Service is conducted with a smile and food is simple and tasty, with the scones and paninis a particular favourite. £

Bia Belfast
An Cultúrlann McAdam Ó Fiaich, 216 Falls Road; tel: 028-9096 4184; www.biabelfast.ie; Mon–Thu 9am–6pm, Fri until 9pm, Sat until 7pm, Sun 10am–4pm.
Located in the Falls Road cultural centre, the atmosphere is welcoming and relaxed. Learn more about West Belfast while sampling the good home-made food. Menus range from snacks and light lunches to full evening meals. Bring your own bottle and expect live music on Saturday nights. £

Mural Art

From harsh political propaganda and monumental historic events to footballing and literary legends, murals on the walls of Northern Ireland's cities tell a fascinating story.

Around 2,000 murals have been documented in Northern Ireland since the 1970s. The sectarian divide between Protestant and Catholic has long been an artistic preoccupation across the North. A century after Protestant William of Orange defeated his Catholic father-in-law James II at the 1690 Battle of the Boyne, artisan coach painters celebrated with gable-end paintings of 'King Billy' riding triumphant on his white horse. The first mural to appear in Belfast was in 1908, again recording William's victory at the Boyne. When partition in 1920 hived off Northern Ireland, triumphalist Orange murals were encouraged, deflecting the attention of poor Protestants from chronic unemployment and miserable housing.

A CHANGING MESSAGE

Until the 1981 IRA hunger strike, nationalists and republicans confined their icons to inside political and sporting clubs. Then, with a growing confidence that they would triumph over Protestants as Protestants had over them, republican murals were born. Protestant murals, on the other hand, had been restricted to references to 1914 gun running, portraits of English royals, biblical prophecies

A cross-community mural on the Newtownards Road.

and portraits of William. Now Protestant paramilitaries saw their role as defenders of the faith. Contemporary military hardware appeared and the murals became increasingly aggressive in their nature. The images underlined the importance of the communities, where the borders lay and whose turf it was.

SECTARIAN MURALS

Along Sandy Row, the Shankill and Newtownards roads, predominantly working-class Protestant heartlands, are loyalist organisation murals which hark back to the B-Specials (a loyalist paramilitary police force disbanded in 1969) and to Cúchulainn, Hound of Ulster, and leader of the 100BC Red Branch Knights.

Meanwhile, in Catholic north and west Belfast, the icons became the lily of the 1916 Easter Rising, Cúchulainn (the republican version), dead hunger strikers and expressions of solidarity with Mexican and Basque revolutionaries. Some read *'saoirse'* (freedom); others, in the past, displayed a mordant wit in such altered traffic signs as 'sniper at work'.

Another noted collection of murals is in the Bogside area of Derry City. Most famous is the 'Free Derry' mural declaring the area's 'independence' from British rule (see page 95).

THE 21ST CENTURY

Travel Belfast's Falls and Shankill roads and you will see some of the most poignant tributes to those who died during the Troubles. Faces of the young look down on passing tourists, a haunting reminder of those harrowing years. The mural of hunger striker Bobby Sands (see page 77), unveiled in the Falls Road in 2000, is one of the most visited in the city. But the peace process has brought new hope to the city and the Falls and Shankill communities are rebuilding their lives.

Murals have evolved as a peaceful, yet powerful, art form, such as the images in east Belfast (see page 86) to C.S. Lewis and George Best, and tributes to one of the most poignant of Belfast icons, the *Titanic*. Murals supporting the Palestinian cause have started to appear in republican West Belfast. Belfast's murals are attracting a new generation of tourists, but remain a compelling reminder of the past and a persuasive tool for the future.

The aluminium exterior of Titanic Belfast.

Tour 9

Titanic Quarter and Eastern Suburbs

From Queen's Island to the home of the Northern Ireland Assembly, this half-day, 10-mile (16km) East Belfast drive reveals many fascinating sights.

The eastern edges of the city have grown up around its shipyard, Harland & Wolff, where a large number of East Belfast's population once worked. Now shipbuilding is overshadowed by the Titanic Quarter. This huge, disparate section, with suburbs, parks and estates, is formless and rambling, but there is much to see, from the Titanic Belfast Visitor Centre to the origins of an unlikely duo of famous sons, C. S. Lewis and George Best.

Highlights

- Titanic Belfast Visitor Centre
- Titanic's Dock and Pump House
- SS Nomadic
- Samson and Goliath
- The Odyssey
- Landmarks of East Belfast's famous sons
- Parliament Buildings and Stormont castle grounds

TITANIC QUARTER

The natural starting point for a tour of the Titanic Quarter is the **Titanic Belfast Visitor Centre** ❶ on Queen's Road (tel: 028-9076 6386; www.titanicbelfast.com, daily Jan–Mar, Oct–Dec 10am–5pm, Apr–May and Sept 9am–6pm, June–Aug 9am–7pm), opened in 2012 to commemorate the 100th anniversary of the liner's sinking. The

Finding your way

It's difficult to navigate your way around the back roads of East Belfast so why not let a Black Taxi take the strain (see page 23). You can customise your tour, whether you want to head for the political murals, the home of *Titanic* or explore the origins of such famous East Belfast sons as C.S. Lewis and George Best. One of the best is Ken Harper (tel: 028-9074 2711; www.harpertaxitours.co.nr).

centre has quickly established itself as a world-class attraction. The building's startling six-storey, bow-shaped, aluminium facade reflects the lines of the ship. Inside, nine interpretative galleries outline the liner's dramatic story as well as the wider theme of Belfast's seafaring and maritime heritage. To the rear of the building are the slipways where the *Titanic* was built, complete with a life-size plan of its promenade deck and a memorial garden.

Titanic's Dock and Pump House

Farther along Queen's Road another atmospheric attraction is the 900ft (275m) -long **Titanic's Dock and Pump House** ❷ where the liner was built. In its time the dry dock was the biggest in the world and now ranks alongside the Titanic Belfast as Northern Ireland's leading attraction. To view the dock and the Edwardian Pump House, you could book onto a private guided tour (tel: 028-9073 7813; www.titanicsdock.com; daily Jan–Mar 10.30am–5pm, Apr–Oct 10am–5pm, Nov–Dec 10am–4pm).

SS *Nomadic*

Beside the visitor centre is the SS ***Nomadic*** ❸ (tel: 028-9027 7652; www.nomadicbelfast.com; daily Apr–May and Sept 10am–6pm, June–Aug until 7pm, Oct–Mar 11am–5pm), tender ship to *Titanic* – known as her 'little sister' – and the last White Star Line ship in existence. It operated as a shuttle ship delivering 142 first-class passengers to *Titanic* in Cherbourg before she set sail across the Atlantic. Interpretative galleries and interactive displays bring alive what it was like for the workers and passengers. The ship is berthed at the Hamilton Graving Dock.

Samson and Goliath

The two massive yellow gantry cranes, named **Samson and Goliath** by all but post-feminists who have rechristened the latter Delilah, dominate the eastern skyline over the Harland and Wolff shipyards at Queen's Island. Today the main work of the yard is in ship repair, structural engineering and design.

The Odyssey

Round the corner, on Queen's Quay, **The Odyssey** ❹ (tel: 028-9045 8806 or 028-9045 7440; www.theodyssey.co.uk) is a multifaceted visitor centre for families. The pavilion offers a variety of ways to keep the kids amused, including the **W5** interactive science and discovery centre (tel: 028-9046 7700; www.

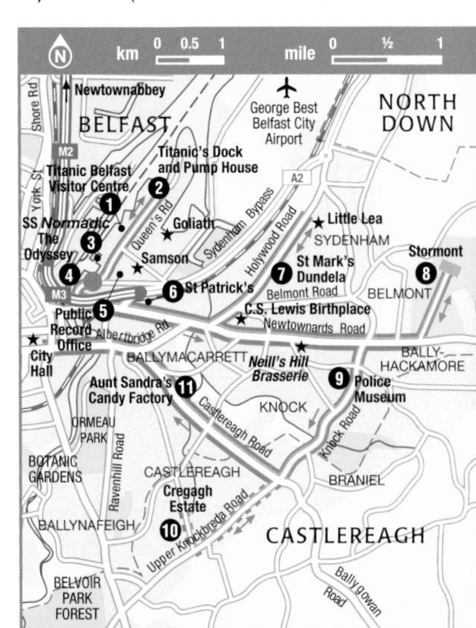

A painted tribute to C.S. Lewis.

w5online.co.uk; Mon–Fri 10am–5pm, Sat 10am–6pm, Sun noon–6pm). The Odyssey also houses a bowling alley, 12 cinema screens, cafés, bars and restaurants, as well as some of Belfast's most popular nightclubs. The adjoining SSE Arena attracts the world's top bands and artists. It transforms into an ice rink for the Belfast Giants ice hockey team.

Public Record Office

Looking for your ancestors? Then this is *the* place to start. A staggering three million documents and 300,000 maps are stored in the archives of the **Public Record Office of Northern Ireland** ❺ on Titanic Boulevard (PRONI; tel: 028-9053 4800; www.proni.gov.uk). Most records date from around 1600 to the present. Helpful staff can assist you in tracking down precious transcripts or elusive records to complete the ancestral family jigsaw.

NEWTOWNARDS ROAD

Head west on Queen's Quay towards Station Street Flyover, take a left at Station Road then east at Middlepath Street (A2) and follow the road as it veers left and becomes Newtownards Road (A20). You can still get a glimpse of East Belfast's prosperous industrial era at the beginning of this road, where much of the old working-class housing has been preserved. On the left stands **St Patrick's** ❻ – the 'Shipyard Church' dating from 1833; note the murals close to loyalist hearts along the side of the road and the **Titanic Mural** painted on the gable end at Dee Street, dedicated to the men and women who lost their lives on that tragic night in 1912.

C.S. LEWIS

Our route detours north onto Holywood Road to nip in and out of streets branching off to the east, the childhood stomping ground of author C.S. Lewis (1898–1963). He wrote fondly of his boyhood years in East Belfast and often yearned for the familiar sounds of the ships' hooters in nearby Belfast Lough. The fifth road on the right, **Dundela Avenue**, is where Lewis was born – a blue plaque marks the spot, where a block of flats now stands. On Sydenham Avenue (third turning after Dundela) is **St Mark's Dundela** ❼ where Lewis saw his fearsome grandfather preach each Sunday. The house he grew up in, **Little Lea** (in whose attic flourished the youthful imagination that led to Narnia), is on Circular Road much further on along Holywood Road, and also marked by a blue plaque. In 2015, his enduring popularity prompted the City Council to create C.S. Lewis Square at the intersection of Connswater and Comber Greenways, with seven sculptures of the characters from *The Lion, the Witch and the Wardrobe*. The square officially opened in November 2016.

STORMONT

Retrace the route to Newtownards Road and head east. After about 1.5 miles (2.5km) you reach the gates of the Parliament Buildings at **Stormont** ❽. Its endless driveway leads through extensive parkland to the Scottish baronial-style castle, bought by the new Northern Ireland government in the early 1920s and opened as the Parliament Building in 1932.

Over the past few years, it has operated as the seat of government. Free guided tours of the striking architecture of Parliament Buildings are available (Mon–Fri 11am and 3pm).

OFF THE KNOCK ROAD

Return the way you came as far as the traffic lights and turn south onto Knock Road. Those with an interest in police uniforms and firearms can visit the **Police Museum** ❾ at No. 65 (tel: 028-9065 0222, ext. 22499; by appointment Mon–Fri 10am–4.30pm; free).

A little further on, take a right turn into Castlereagh Road, where our tour continues. George Best fans might carry on for another quarter mile or so to the **Cregagh Estate** ❿ and his childhood home at No. 16 Burren Way (www.georgebesthouse.com), which is now available to rent as a holiday house. A mural depicting George decorates the wall at the end of Burren Way. The best way to gain inside information remains to take one of the taxi tours (see page 23).

At 60 Castlereagh Road, children can watch sweets and chocolates being made in the traditional way at **Aunt Sandra's Candy Factory** ⓫ (tel: 028-9073 2868; www.auntsandras.com; Mon–Sat 9am–5.30pm, Sun 10am–5pm). At the end of the road, bear west onto Albert Bridge Road and head back to the city.

Eating Out

Bennetts
4 Belmont Road; tel: 028-9065 6590; www.bennettsonbelmont.com; Mon–Thu 8am–9pm, Fri–Sat 8am–10pm, Sun 9am–5pm.
Just off Holywood Road, this hidden gem is a little cramped but it's always busy. The fare is fresh, simple and good value. £

Marco Pierre White Steakhouse Bar & Grill
Park Avenue Hotel, 158 Holywood Road; tel: 028-9065 6520; www.parkavenuehotel.co.uk; Mon–Thu 6–9pm, Fri–Sat 5–10pm, Sun noon–8pm.
As Marco Pierre White's only outpost in Northern Ireland, this restaurant has built a loyal following. Expect great steaks and an excellent wine and cocktail list. Located in the four-star Park Avenue Hotel, which has been in the same family since 1959. ££

Neill's Hill Brasserie
229 Upper Newtownards Road; tel: 028-9065 0079; www.neillshill.com; Mon–Thu 10am–9.30pm, Fri 10am–10pm, Sat 9.30am–10pm, Sun 10am–8.30pm.
Formerly called Aldens, this restaurant has reinvented itself as a casual brasserie. Main courses include pan-roasted salmon or sea bass from Walter Ewing, Belfast's number one fish supplier. ££

Stoker's Halt
199 Upper Newtownards Road; tel: 028-9092 1920; www.stokershalt.com; daily noon–9pm.
Slow-braised beef and Guinness pie, blackened chorizo chicken, crumbed carrot-courgette burger, and rib-eye and sirloin steaks all feature, prepared and served with flair. £–££

The interlocking basalt columns of the Giant's Causeway.

Tour 10

Coastal Causeway to Derry

This spectacular 132-mile (212km) route along the Antrim coast encompasses the Giant's Causeway and dramatic rugged cliffs, then turns inland to the walled city of Derry.

For many, a drive along the Antrim Coast Road, known as the Causeway Coastal Route, to the Giant's Causeway would be enough for one day, and there is the option of taking one of the many bus tours that cover the same route. But for those who want to explore a bit more, head on to Derry, also called Londonderry. To make the most of the complete tour, spend a night there and have a proper look round the next morning. Literature buffs should make their last stop Bellaghy, where Seamus Heaney grew up, to visit the sparkling new Seamus Heaney HomePlace (see page 96). Situated midway between Derry and Belfast, this informative exhibition and arts centre could be taken in on a return journey to Belfast.

Highlights

- Carrickfergus
- Causeway Coastal Route
- Giant's Causeway
- Bushmills Distillery
- Dunluce Castle
- Derry's walls and Peace Bridge
- Derry's Guildhall
- Seamus Heaney HomePlace

NORTH OF BELFAST

Take the A2 north out of the city, through the well-to-do suburbs of Whiteabbey and Greenisland, and on to **Carrickfergus ❶**, a market town 12 miles (19km) north along the A2. Its big synthetic-fibre plants have gone, but the imposing 13th-century **Nor-**

man **Carrickfergus Castle** (Marine Highway; tel: 028-9335 1273; daily 10am–6pm), built on top of a rock ledge, is still in excellent shape (see page 89). It is a real castle, with a portcullis, ramparts looking out over the sea, and chilling dungeons. Looking to the age of leisure, the town's marina has 300 berths. The parish church of St Nicholas (with stained-glass windows to Santa Claus) is 12th century.

In Antrim Street, **Carrickfergus Museum** (tel: 028-9335 8049; Apr–Sept Mon–Fri 10am–6pm, Sat until 4pm, Oct–Mar until 5pm; free) outlines the town's history. **Flame!** (44 Irish Quarter West; tel: 028-9336 9575; www.flamegasworks.co.uk; 2–5pm May–Aug Sun–Fri, Sept Mon–Fri) is Ireland's only gasworks museum. About a mile (2km) to the east, the **Andrew Jackson Cottage** (Boneybefore; tel: 028-9335 8241; by appointment with Carrickfergus Visitor's Centre; free) is a reconstruction of the thatched cottage home of Andrew Jackson, seventh president of the United States.

Tales of Carrickfergus

Carrickfergus, celebrated in song by Van Morrison, has good stories to tell. Its castle was besieged for a year in 1315 by Edward Bruce's Scottish invaders. William of Orange first set foot on Irish soil here on his way to defeat James II at the Battle of the Boyne in 1690. The French briefly captured the town in 1760.

Unspoilt beaches

The countryside north of Carrickfergus becomes rich meadowland, with the sleepy seaside town of **Whitehead**, base for the Railway Preservation Society of Ireland, from where occasional steam excursions run. The town nestles at the mouth of the lough, with a seashore walk to the Black Head lighthouse. Beyond begins the peninsula of **Island Magee**, with unspoilt beaches and caves, which wraps around Larne Lough. A highlight of the peninsula is the historic **Gobbins cliff**

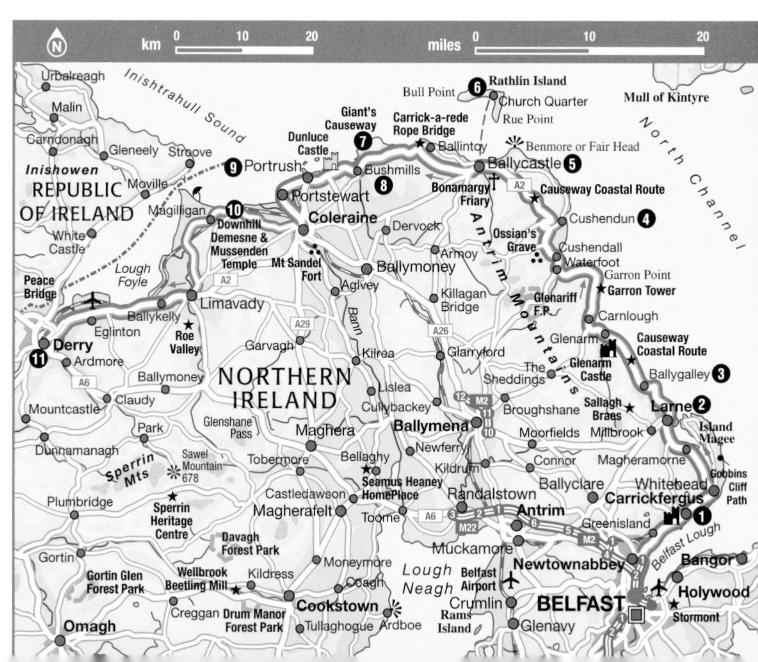

The view from the Antrim coast road.

path, a dramatic coastal walk cut into the rock and restored in a £6m project that comes complete with a new stainless-steel staircase linking a half-mile path with the creation of a new cliff-top path. From here, the road runs into unlovely **Larne** ❷, a port with frequent ferries to and from Stranraer in Scotland (70 minutes away). The **Larne Museum and Arts Centre** (2 Victoria Road; tel: 028-2827 9482; Mon–Sat 10am–4.30pm; free) has displays reflecting the history and heritage of the area.

CAUSEWAY COASTAL ROUTE

The rewards of continuing along the coast are spectacular views of brown moorlands, white limestone, black basalt, red sandstone and blue sea. A notable engineering achievement, it is explained in the Larne Visitor Information Centre (Narrow Gauge Road; tel: 028-2826 2495; Mon–Fri 9am–5pm, Sat 10am–4pm, Sun 11am–3pm, Oct–Mar closed Sun; free). The road, designed in 1834 by Sir Charles Lanyon, opened up an area whose inhabitants had previously found it easier to travel by sea to Scotland than overland to the rest of Ireland.

Ballygalley

Ballygalley ❸, at the start of the scenic drive, has a 1625 fortified mansion (now a hotel) and, inland, a well-preserved mill and pottery. White Bay is a picnic area around which small fossils can be found. **Glenarm** has a beautiful park adjoining a fussy castle, home of the earls of Antrim. **Carnlough** has a fine harbour and, running over its main street, a white bridge built in 1854 to carry limestone from the quarries to waiting boats. The Londonderry Arms hotel retains the charms of an old coaching inn.

The Glens

Next you reach **Waterfoot**, which is at the entrance to Glenariff Glen, a deep wooded gorge dubbed by Thackeray 'Switzerland in miniature'. Wild flowers carpet the upper glen in spring and early summer, and rustic bridges carry walkers over the Glenariff River, past postcard-pretty waterfalls.

About 1.5 miles (2km) to the north, **Cushendall**, 'capital of the glens', was created largely by a wealthy 19th-century landowner, Francis Turnley. His most striking structure was the four-storey red sandstone Curfew Tower, built as 'a place of confinement

Crashing waves at Ballycastle.

for idlers and rioters'. The village has a good beach and is a popular sailing centre. Just to the north is Layde Old Church, dating from the 13th century and containing some ancient vaults. Six miles (10km) further on you can loop round on the B92 to **Cushendun** ❹, a village of attractive white cottages, graceful old houses and friendly pubs, protected by the National Trust.

THE NORTHERN COAST

Still following the Causeway Coastal Route you cross the towering Glendun Viaduct (1839), and just before arriving in Ballycastle, pass the ruins of Bonamargy Friary, founded around 1500. A vault contains the massive coffins of several MacDonnell chieftains who successfully rebuffed the forces of Queen Elizabeth I.

Ballycastle

The best time to visit **Ballycastle** ❺ is during the Auld Lammas Fair, held on the last Monday and Tuesday of August. Then this unspoilt town turns into one throbbing marketplace as farmers with impenetrable accents bring their livestock in from the glens and hundreds of stalls sell souvenirs, bric-a-brac, dulse (dried, edible seaweed) and yellowman (a sweet confectionery). The big attraction is the *craic* – pronounced 'crack' (a Scots-Irish word for talk, enlivened by a drop of Bushmills). It's great fun and an authentic folk event. The **Ballycastle Museum** (Castle Street; tel: 028-2076 2942; July–Aug daily 10am–6pm, Apr–May and Sept Fri–Sat 10am–6pm, Sun noon–4pm; free) concentrates on the folk history of the Glens.

A seafront memorial marks the spot where, in 1898, Guglielmo Marconi

The Giant's Causeway

The Giant's Causeway Visitor Experience (http://giantscausewaytickets.com) is sunken into the ground, blending effectively into the landscape and ensuring that the indigenous grasses on the roof restore the natural ridgeline and provide a habitat for wildlife. Special environmental features include water-permeable paving and rainwater harvesting. Visitors are encouraged to help the environment by parking in Bushmills and opting for the park and ride service.

The sunken visitor centre.

first seriously tested wireless telegraphy. He made his historic transmission between here and **Rathlin Island** ❻, 8 miles (13km) off the coast towards Scotland. The boomerang-shaped island, whose population has slumped from 2,000 to 100 since 1850, attracts geologists, botanists and birdwatchers; a reserve (tel: 028-2076 3948) monitors an estimated 250,000 birds of 175 species. There is one pub, a hotel, guesthouse and youth hostel – but no policeman, and no need for one. A ferry (tel: 028-2076 9299; www.rathlinballycastleferry.com; daily year-round; reservations advised) makes the journey from Ballycastle in 45 minutes. In the summer (July–Sept) a high-speed catamaran cuts the crossing time to 25 minutes with six round-trips daily.

Carrick-a-rede Rope Bridge

Carry on along the Causeway Coastal Route, which diverts west off the A2 to the **Carrick-a-rede Rope Bridge** (tel: 028-2076 9839; Mar–Oct daily 10am–6pm, Nov–Feb 10.30am–3.30pm), over an 80ft (24m) chasm to an island salmon fishery (see box). It's worth crossing the bridge for the view of the crashing waves, but it is a good 0.5 miles (1km) from the car park. Back on the road past Whitepark Bay is Dunseverick Castle, the slight remains of a 6th-century fortress perched on a crag overlooking a fishing harbour. Follow the signs to the Giant's Causeway.

Exhilarating bridge

The Carrick-a-rede Rope Bridge provides a novel way to get an alternative view of the spectacular coastline. Spare a thought for the salmon fishermen who traversed this chasm, braving a bridge of widely spaced wooden slats and a single rope handrail. Today you get two handrails and a more substantial suspension bridge. Old photographs even show people performing stunts, such as handstands on a chair in the middle and riding across on a bicycle.

The Giant's Causeway

Dunseverick Castle is at the eastern end of the **Giant's Causeway** ❼, an astonishing assembly, discovered only in 1692, of more than 40,000 basalt columns, mostly perfect hexagons formed by the cooling of molten lava. The formal approach is via the Giant's Causeway Visitor Experience (tel: 028-2073 2844; http://giantscausewaytickets.com; car park charge included in

The prismatic shapes of the spectacular Giant's Causeway.

Crossing the Carrick-a-rede rope bridge.

admission ticket) 2 miles (3km) north of Bushmills on the B146. The sparkling new glass-fronted visitor centre is made of locally quarried basalt (see page 91). A minibus provides wheelchair access to the Causeway. For a small fee anyone can take the shuttlebus, but it is a lovely walk down to the rocks and there are opportunities for longer walks along the coast. Please note in high summer the causeway is extremely busy – you are strongly advised to book online for a date and time slot.

One of the most pleasant ways to reach the Giant's Causeway is on the **Giant's Causeway and Bushmills Railway** steam train (tel: 028-2073 2844; July–Aug and Easter daily, Mar–Oct Sat–Sun), from Bushmills, which is where the route continues, following the coastal route, the A2.

The world's oldest distillery

The distillery at **Bushmills** ❽ (Distillery Road; tel: 028-2073 3218; www.bushmills.com; guided tours: Mar–Oct Mon–Sat 9.15am–4.45pm, Sun noon–4.45pm, Nov–Feb Mon–Sat 10am–4.45pm, Sun noon–4.45pm) a couple of miles away, has the world's oldest whiskey-making licence (1608). Old Bushmills, Black Bush and Bushmills Malt, made from local barley and the water that flows by in St Columb's Rill, can be tasted after a tour.

About 2 miles (3km) along the coast road are the romantic remains of **Dunluce Castle** (tel: 028-2073 1938; Apr–Sept daily 10am–6pm, Oct–Mar until 4pm). Poised on a rocky headland, the dramatic 14th-century stronghold was featured in HBO's *Game of Thrones*. It was abandoned in 1641, two years after part of the kitchen collapsed into the sea during a storm, carrying many of the servants to their deaths. In the graveyard of the adjacent ruined church are buried sailors from the Spanish Armada galleass *Girona*, wrecked on nearby rocks

Barrels at Bushmills Distillery.

Derry, on the River Foyle.

in 1588. The castle was once owned by Sir Winston Churchill.

PORTRUSH AND PORTSTEWART

Next along the coast are two seaside resorts. **Portrush** ❾ is the brasher, with amusement arcades, burger bars, karaoke pubs, souvenir shops, a children's play park, boat trips for sea fishing and viewing the Causeway, and two championship golf courses.

Portstewart is the quieter, a tidy Victorian town with a huge strand, popular with anglers for its excellent beach casting. Long-distance walkers can pick up the North Antrim Coast Path at Portstewart Strand; it forms part of the Ulster Way and extends east for 40 miles (64km) to Murlough Bay. The road bypasses **Coleraine**, a busy market and university town.

Portrush pleasures

Portrush (tel: 028-7082 3600) has seashore exhibits and rock-pool creatures in a touch tank. For an alternative, fun-filled family experience, you can while away a morning or afternoon at the long-established Barry's Amusements (tel: 028-7082 2340; www.barrysamusements.com) where dodgems and the thrill of the big dipper are the main attractions.

THE ROAD TO DERRY

Continue on the A2 towards Derry City, 37 miles (60km) via the coastal route. On a windswept headland is **Downhill Demesne** ❿ (Castlerock; tel: 028-7084 8728; Apr–Sept daily 10am–5pm), concealing the ruins of Downhill Castle and Hezlett House. Here too is **Mussenden Temple**, perched on a cliff, which housed an eccentric bishop's library; it was inspired by the temples of Vesta at Tivoli and Rome. Downhill Forest has lovely walks and waterfalls.

Benone Beach, part of **Magilligan Strand**, is one of Ireland's best, with golf, tennis and heated pools available at its excellent adjoining Tourist Complex (tel: 028-7775 0555).

Follow the A2 to Limavady and on to Derry, where you might consider staying the night.

DERRY CITY

Derry ⓫, finely situated on the River Foyle, is famously friendly. Even its sectarian conflicts are far less implacable than Belfast's. The 19th-century Scottish historian Thomas Carlyle called it 'the prettiest looking town I have seen in Ireland'. The Troubles seriously scarred it but it has been well refurbished. Since 2011 the city's major public buildings such as St. Columb's Cathedral, the Guildhall, and its museums and churches have emerged from a beautification programme. The

Bogside artists

A good way to experience the political history of the Bogside is to join a tour of the dramatic murals. Guided tours of all 12 murals, known collectively as 'The People's Gallery', are available and you learn more of the history that inspired the artists. You won't hear the stories elsewhere: these are straight from the horse's mouth.

The historic Derry walls.

spectacular **Peace Bridge** across the Foyle opened in 2011 linking the west bank with Ebrington Square, a redeveloped military parade ground now turned into an arts hub hosting concerts and other events. In 2013 it was one of the main centres for the year-long UK City of Culture programme during which Derry trumpeted its artistic credentials to a wider world and which has left an important legacy.

The city's growth was financed by London guilds, which in 1613 began creating the last walled city in Europe. You can see traces of its former economic confidence in the ornamental facades of the old shirt-making factories, which provided the city with its livelihood. The walls, 20ft (6m) thick and complete with watchtowers and cannon, are marvellously intact (tel: 028-7134 7176 for tours; www.derrywalls.com).

Two 17th-century sieges failed to breach the walls. Some say the city still has a siege mentality, a theory reinforced by the IRA's daubed slogan 'You are now entering Free Derry'. This was the name given to the Bogside (see page 95), a densely populated Catholic housing estate, when its inhabitants barricaded it against the police in 1969. Their grievances were old ones. For more on the civil rights movement

A message painted on the wall of a house in Bogside.

and the story of Bloody Sunday, visit the **Museum of Free Derry** (55 Glenfada Park, Bogside; tel: 028-7136 0880; www.museumoffreederry.org; Mon–Fri 9.30am–4.30pm, also Sat 1–4pm Apr–Sept and Sun 1–4pm July–Sept).

The most famous siege took place in 1689, when the Catholic forces of James II blockaded the Protestant supporters of William of Orange for 15 weeks, almost forcing them into submission. About 7,000 of the 30,000 people packed within the city's walls died of disease or starvation. One member of the besieged garrison chillingly recorded the selling prices of horseflesh, dogs' heads, cats, and rats 'fattened by eating the bodies of the slain Irish'. The city's eventual relief is depicted in the memorial window of St Columb's Cathedral, a graceful 17th-century Anglican church.

Tower Museum

The **Tower Museum** (Union Hall Place; tel: 028-7137 2411; www.derrycity.gov.uk/museums; daily 10am–5.30pm) skilfully uses audiovisuals and photography to tell the city's turbulent history from both sides of the sectarian divide.

Inside the Tower Museum.

Around the city

Streets from the city's original four gates converge on The Diamond, a square-shaped marketplace at the top of steep Shipquay Street. At the bottom, the rejuvenated **Guildhall** (Guildhall Street; tel: 028-7137 6510; daily 10am–5.30pm; free) benefitted from a three-year £10-million makeover (completed in 2013) and is an outstanding example of the city's impressive architecture. It has been refashioned as a tourist information point with permanent touch-screen displays explaining the building's special features.

Behind the Guildhall is Derry Quay, celebrated in song by thousands of emigrants who sailed down the Foyle, bound for a new life in America.

Literary detour

Take the A6 out of Derry into the mid-Ulster countryside for 38 miles (65km) to the village of Bellaghy, where the late poet and Nobel laureate Seamus Heaney grew up. Heaney's poetry was massively inspired by the surrounding countryside and frequently evoked rural life. **Seamus Heaney HomePlace** (45 Main Street; tel. 028-7938 7444; www.seamusheaneyhome.com; Mon–Sat 10am–5pm, Sun 1–5pm) is a sleek arts centre opened in 2016, with a permanent exhibition on Heaney's life, a café, a theatre and a full cultural programme. Housed in a former police barracks that has been reimagined into a £4.25-million modernist space, the centre enjoys stunning rural views. Its location, a 45-minute drive from either Derry or Belfast, makes it a convenient day trip from either city.

Eating Out

Ballycastle

The Cellar Restaurant

11b The Diamond; tel: 028-2076 3037; www.cellarballycastle.com; Sept–May Mon–Fri and Sun 5–9.30pm, Sat noon–10pm, June–July daily noon–10pm.
Plenty of atmosphere at this cosy restaurant with its vaulted ceiling and individual eating areas. Seafood is the speciality, but meat lovers will not be disappointed with some excellent local beef. ££–£££

Bushmills

Bushmills Inn

9 Dunluce Road; tel: 028-2073 3000; www.bushmillsinn.com; daily noon–5pm and 6–9.30pm, Sun lunch noon–3pm.
Ever-popular 19th-century coaching inn where traditional dishes are given the Bushmills twist on this true Ulster menu. Try the Kilhorne Bay crab and prawns or the Finnebrogue venison. £££

Tartine

Distillers Arms, 140 Main Street; tel: 028-2073 1044; www.distillersarms.com; Thu–Fri and Sun 5–8.30pm, Sat until 9.30pm, also Sun noon–2.15pm.
A contemporary restaurant in the former distillery pub. The menu features succulent local venison, lamb, steak and seafood. Great-value Sunday lunch and 'Dinner Madness' (two-course early bird, 5–6.30pm) menu. ££–£££

Carnlough

Londonderry Arms Hotel

20 Harbour Road; tel: 028-2888 5255; www.glensofantrim.com; daily noon–9pm.
A traditional inn where the choice ranges from bar meals in the Coach House Bistro to an old-fashioned high tea or more elaborate dinner in the Frances Anne Tapestry restaurant. Expect to find fish, duck, chicken, steak and pork along with salads and vegetarian dishes. ££–£££

Cushendall

Harry's Restaurant

23 Mill Street; tel: 028-2177 2022; www.harrysrestaurant.com; daily noon–9pm.
A good stop for a quick bite, serving typical bistro/pub grub-style food. Good-value meals, including huge roasts, are served in the downstairs bar, while more refined cuisine can be found upstairs. £–££

Derry

Browns Restaurant

1–2 Bond's Hill; 028-7134 5180; www.brownsrestaurant.com; Tue–Fri noon–2.30pm, Tue–Sat 5.30pm–late, Sun 10.30am–3pm.
This well-respected establishment also has a Champagne lounge. Both the ambience and the food are good – insiders recommend the chargrilled fillet of beef. £££

Café del Mondo

29 Craft Village, off Shipquay Street; tel: 028-7136 6877; café Mon–Sat 9am–6pm, Sun noon–5pm; restaurant Tue–Sat 6–11pm.
The constantly busy del Mondo operates as a café during the day and in the evening transforms itself into a licensed restaurant. Freshly prepared organic food and free-trade produce are priorities. A typical menu may include hot and sweet butternut squash, corn-fed Irish chicken or pan-fried sea bass. ££

Giant's Causeway

The Smugglers Inn

306 Whitepark Road; tel: 028-2073 1577; www.smugglersinnireland.com; daily noon–3pm and 4.30–9pm.
Perfectly placed on the Causeway Coastal Route; stop for a drink or eat in the à la carte Girona Restaurant or the more casual Benbow Bistro. Beef and Guinness pie is one of the favourite choices. ££

Step back in time at the Ulster-American Folk Park.

Tour 11

Across Three Counties

Covering 150 miles (240km), this one-day tour of three counties encompasses some of the most popular attractions in Northern Ireland, plus a brief trip into the Republic.

County Tyrone, in the heart of Northern Ireland, is home to the majestic Sperrin Mountains, forests and rivers, and is favoured by hill walkers and anglers. Fermanagh encompasses a delightful profusion of waterways, the most visited being Lough Erne. The most northerly point in Ireland is in the Republic – don't forget euros as you cross the border – in County Donegal. It's an open, unspoilt region, popular with holidaymakers. If you have time, consider staying overnight along the route.

Highlights

- Ulster-American Folk Park
- Lough Erne
- Marble Arch Caves
- Lough Navar Forest Park
- Castle Caldwell
- Belleek
- Donegal

COUNTY TYRONE

Thirteen miles (21km) southwest of **Derry City**, in County Tyrone on the A5, is **Strabane** ❶, a border town paired with Lifford on the Donegal side. The Tourist Information Centre (Railway Street, Mon–Sat 9–5pm) has details of attractions in the town and surrounding area. In Dergalt, 2 miles (3km) southeast, signposted off the B47, is a whitewashed cottage, ancestral home of US president Woodrow Wilson (tel: 028-7138 4444; July–Aug Tue–Sun 2–5pm; free).

Recreation of an old Ulster street, Ulster-American Folk Park.

Sion Mills, 3 miles (5km) south of Strabane, is a planned model village whose name betrays its origins. The linen-workers' cottages are charming. The parish Church of the Good Shepherd is a striking Italian-style edifice, contrasting with the modernist St Teresa's Catholic Church, whose slate facade depicts the Last Supper by Irish sculptor Oisin Kelly. Continue along the A5 to the Ulster-American Folk Park.

Ulster-American Folk Park

Thomas Mellon, who emigrated to Pittsburgh at the age of five in 1818, went on to found a great industrial and banking empire. His descendants, having traced their family roots to 4 miles (6km) north of Omagh, off the A5, endowed the **Ulster-American Folk Park** ❷ (tel: 028-8224 3292; www.nmni.com; Mar–June and Sept Tue–Sun 10am–5pm, July–Aug daily 10am–5pm, Oct–Feb Tue–Fri 10am–4pm, Sat–Sun 11am–4pm) on the site at Camphill. An indoor exhibit re-creates the main street of an Ulster town a century ago, its hardware shop displaying foot warmers and lamp wicks, its medical hall containing Bishop's Granular Effervescent Citrate of Magnesia. A replica of an emigrant ship links the continents. History comes to life on special occasions (such as US Independence Day) when 'living history' actors re-create battles, while others demonstrate traditional cooking and craft skills. The Mellon Centre for Migration Studies on the site has a reference library open for research. There is also a good café and picnic areas.

County town

As you drive into **Omagh** ❸, the religious fragmentation of Northern Ireland is apparent in the abundance of churches. The joining of the rivers Camowen and Drumragh to form the Strule make the location pleasant enough, but Omagh is more a town for living in than for visiting.

Locals still recall the day in August 1998 when a car exploded in the town, killing 31 people. On the 10th anniversary of the bombing, a poignant

Enniskillen Castle.

memorial was opened (www.omagh bombmemorial.com).

COUNTY FERNANAGH

From Omagh take the A32 to the county town of Fermanagh, **Enniskillen** ❹, a Protestant stronghold since Tudor times, built on an island between two channels of the River Erne as it flows from Upper to Lower **Lough Erne**. Although something of a traffic bottleneck, in summer you can get away from it all by taking one of the pleasure boats that ply the lakes (MV *Kestrel*, Round O Quay; tel: 028-6632 2882; www.ernetoursltd.com; 2.15pm and 4.15pm June–Aug daily, May, Sept–Oct Tue, Sat–Sun). Three miles (5km) north of the town at the A32/B82 junction, **Devenish Island** is the best known of the lough's 97 islands for its elaborate and well-preserved tower, which can be climbed by internal ladders. Close by are the decorative ruins of the 12th-century Augustinian Abbey of St Mary. In June 2013 a £1.2-million 'Fermanagh facelift' saw the locality being spruced up for the G8 summit where the world leaders stayed for several days at the Lough Erne Resort Hotel.

Monumental view

If you have the energy to climb 108 steps to the top of Cole's Monument in Forthill Park, Enniskillen, you will get a stunning view of the surrounding area from the viewing platform (tel: 028-6632 3110; Apr–Sept 1.30–3pm; tickets from the Tourist Information Centre).

Enniskillen town

The town's strategic importance is shown by **Enniskillen Castle** (tel: 028-6632 5000; www.enniskillencastle.co.uk; June–Sept Mon–Fri 9.30am–5pm, Sat–Sun 11am–5pm), the earliest parts dating from the 15th century. The castle houses the Fermanagh County Museum, focusing on local history, and the Inniskillings Museum, with exhibits on military history and weaponry.

Enniskillen is rich in small bakeries and butchers' shops, and there's a gossipy atmosphere as farmers mix with townsfolk in Blakes of the Hollow on Church Street (tel. 028-6632 2143; http://blakesofthehollow.com), one of the North's finest pubs.

Two miles (3km) east of Enniskillen on the A4 is Ireland's finest classical mansion, **Castle Coole** (tel: 028-6632 2690; www.nationaltrust.org.uk; house: 11am–5pm May–Sept daily, Mar–Apr Sat–Sun; grounds: daily 10am–dusk).

Marble Arch Caves

'Over 300 million years of history' is the slogan used to promote **Marble Arch Caves** ❺ (Marlbank; tel: 028-6634 8855; www.marblearchcavesgeopark.com; Apr–June and Sept daily 10am–4.30pm, July–Aug until 5pm, Oct 11am–3pm, weather permitting), one of the most visited sights in Ireland. Located 12 miles (20km) southwest of Enniskillen, the caves are reached by following the A4 southwest for 3 miles (5km), then branching off on the A32 and following signposts towards Swanlinbar. They are an extensive network of limestone chambers, containing remarkable stalactites. A 75-minute tour includes an underground boat journey. There's also a café and a shop.

Florence Court

Four miles (6km) east of the caves is a beautiful 18th-century mansion, **Florence Court** ❻ (tel: 028-6634 8249; www.nationaltrust.org.uk; house: May–Sept daily 11am–5pm, Mar–Apr and Oct Sat–Sun only; grounds: daily 10am–dusk). In the interior are fine rococo plasterwork and 18th-century furniture. The grounds include an ice-house, a water-powered sawmill and a walled garden.

LOUGH ERNE

Rejoin the A32 and take the A4 back to Enniskillen for a tour of Lower Lough Erne by road or boat. Follow the A46 north to Tully, with a well-preserved 17th-century castle and gardens. Inland from here take the B81 to Derrygonnelly and follow signs for a 7-mile (11km) drive through **Lough Navar Forest Park** ❼ (daily 10am–sunset all year). There are panoramic views of the lough, Donegal Bay and the Blue Stack and Sperrin mountains from the Magho Cliffs, which rise to 1,000ft (304m). Car parking, picnic areas, viewpoints and a short walk are available. Back on the A46, you can take a small detour north at Rosscor to join the A47 to visit **Castle Caldwell** ❽ 5 miles (8km) east.

This ruined 16th-century castle by the loughside is the centrepiece of a Forest Park (tel: 028-6634 3165; daily dawn–dusk; free), popular with picnickers and birdwatchers. Both Castle Caldwell and Castle Archdale (see box) are part of tours from Ecotourism Ireland (www.ecotourismireland.ie), which provides a large number of eco-friendly holiday options in Fer-

Castle Archdale

A centre for eco-tours, Castle Archdale Country Park (Countryside Centre: tel: 028-6862 1588; Apr–Sept daily 10am–6pm; park: daily 9am–dusk; free) on the east shore has pony trekking, boating and 230 acres (90 hectares) of lovely parkland with some wonderful walks and cycle rides. A ferry departs from Castle Archdale marina for White Island, famed for its 12th-century church, with eight mysterious pagan statues.

Lough Navar Forest Park sits on the shores of lower Lough Erne.

Making the finishing touches at Belleek pottery.

managh and elsewhere. Return along the A47 to Belleek.

Belleek

The border touches the River Erne again at **Belleek** ❾. The village is famous for its lustrous pottery, manufactured from felspar imported from Norway. The Visitor Centre (tel: 028-6865 8501; www.belleekpottery.ie; Jan–Feb Mon–Fri 9am–5.30pm, Mar–June and Oct–Dec Mon–Fri 9am–5.30pm, Sat 10am–5.30pm, Sun 2–5.30pm, July–Sept Mon–Fri 9am–6pm, Sat 10am–6pm, Sun noon–5.30; free) at the distinctive 1893 factory building is another of Ireland's most popular attractions.

COUNTY DONEGAL

Leaving Belleek, continue north to County Donegal, where you reach the Republic, taking the N3 to the bypassed **Ballyshannon**, then the N15 to the lively county town of **Donegal** ❿, with a busy triangular 'Diamond' market square, congested with tourist traffic all summer. The town's **castle** (tel: 074-972 2405; Mar–Oct Mon–Sun 10am–6pm, Nov–Feb Thu–Mon 9.30am–4.30pm), once an O'Donnell stronghold, was redesigned by planters who took over the land after the O'Donnells were deported in the 'Flight of the Earls' at the turn of the 17th century. In the now-ruined Franciscan abbey, on the Eske estuary, monks compiled *The Annals of the Four Masters* in the 1630s, tracing Ireland's ancient history.

Apart from tourism, the weaving and making up of tweeds is the main industry, and Magee's (www.magee1866.com), the largest shop, is the principal outlet. A mile (1.6km) south on the R267, Donegal Craft Village (tel: 074-972 2225; www.donegalcraftvillage.com) demonstrates weaving and other crafts.

Taking the N15 out of Donegal, and passing Lough Eske to the west, the route enters the rugged, dramatic **Barnesmore Gap**. Continue past Lough Mourne, through Ballybofey and north on the N13 to **Letterkenny** ⓫, a vibrant town on the River Swilly, whose most prominent landmark is the cathedral, built in neo-Gothic style by local masons, using Donegal stone.

Eating Out

Belleek

The Thatch

20 Main Street; tel: 028-6865 8181; Mon–Sat 9am–5pm (from 10am in winter).

This coffee shop, dating from the 18th century, is the only thatched building remaining in the county. It has been serving home-made food since the early 1900s. Today's options include baked potatoes, sandwiches, soups and scrumptious cakes and muffins. £

Donegal

Aroma

The Craft Village; tel: 074-972 3222; Mon–Sat 9.30am–5.30pm (lunch noon–4pm).

Everything is prepared and baked daily on the premises at this coffee shop at the craft centre. Plenty of choice for a coffee break, lunch or afternoon tea; particularly good are the Mexican *chimichangas* and *quesadillas*, and the set lunch menus are good value. £–££

Just one of the many bars in Donegal.

Olde Castle Bar & Red Hugh's Restaurant

Castle Street, Milltown; tel: 074-972 1262; www.oldecastlebar.com; daily bar food noon–9pm, dinner 6–9.15pm.

Described as Donegal's leading seafood restaurant, this attractive place has won several awards. Push the boat out for the seafood platter for two or try the Donegal oysters or mussels. £££

Enniskillen

Café Merlot

6 Church Street; tel: 028-6632 0918; http://cafemerlot.co.uk; daily noon–3pm, 5–9pm.

Noted for its reliable cooking and atmospheric vaulted dining, this informal bistro attracts the crowds, especially the two-course early bird. The menu ranges from risotto and antipasti to Dover sole and pheasant. £–££

Letterkenny

Lemon Tree Restaurant

39 Lower Main Street; tel 074-912 5788; www.thelemontreerestaurant.com; daily 5–9.30pm, also Sun lunch 1–2.30pm.

This is an inviting place offering an excellent Irish-sourced menu on which seafood is dominant: monkfish, mackerel, cod and seabass are all on offer. Good-value Early Bird menu. ££–£££

Omagh

Philly's Phinest Diner

12 Bridge Street; tel: 075-6324 4615; Mon–Sat 11–5pm, Sun noon–3pm.

Ireland's only food outlet dedicated to the Philly Cheese Steak. Famous throughout the country for their mouth-watering creations, served in a variety of styles including double cheesesteaks and pizza cheesesteaks with a side of loaded pulled-pork nachos. £

Strabane

Oysters

37 Patrick Street; tel: 028-7138 2690; www.oystersrestaurant.co.uk; daily noon–9.30pm, Sat until 10pm).

Classic dishes get a contemporary makeover at this popular restaurant. Seafood such as blackened salmon and fresh lobster are highlights here, all locally sourced. ££

The Mourne Mountains meet the sea at Newcastle.

Tour 12

Armagh and the Mourne Mountains

Covering 120 miles (194km), this is a one-day tour of captivating contrasts: from outer city suburbs to stunning mountain scenery.

County Armagh is called the 'Apple Orchard of Ireland', known for its National Trust properties, neat villages and country lanes. As we move into County Down, the Mourne Mountains offer wonderful outdoor recreation and the most stunning scenery Northern Ireland has to offer.

Highlights

- Lough Neagh Discovery Centre
- Armagh
- Gosford Forest Park
- Mourne Mountains
- Rostrevor

ROAD TO ARMAGH

Take the A1 south from Belfast to the lively city of **Lisburn** ❶, which has an informative **Museum and Irish Linen Centre** (Market Square; tel: 028-9266 3377; www.lisburnmuseum.com; Mon–Sat 9.30am–5pm; free).

From Lisburn take the A3 towards Armagh, making a short detour to **Lough Neagh Discovery Centre** ❷ (tel: 028-3832 2205; www.oxfordisland.com; Mon–Fri 9am–5pm, Sat–Sun 10am–5pm; free) on Oxford Island. The lough is 17 miles long by 11 miles wide (27km by 18km), the largest inland sheet of water in the British Isles.

Because of its marshy edges, it has few access points – one reason it has remained one of Western Europe's most important bird habitats. The best way to explore is aboard *The Maid of Antrim* (tel: 028-9447 3999; www.loughneaghcruises.co.uk; Sunday cruises depart Antrim marina Apr–Oct hourly, noon–5.00pm). Facilities for sailing and water-skiing have been developed at the marina.

ARMAGH CITY

Continue on the A3 to **Armagh ❸**, which symbolises many of Northern Ireland's past conflicts. Its two striking cathedrals – one Protestant, one Catholic and both called St Patrick's – sit on opposite hills, still causing a divide among the community.

At one end of an oval Mall is a classical courthouse, at the other a former jailhouse. The Ionic-pillared **County Museum** (The Mall; tel: 028-3752 3070; www.nmni.com; Mon–Fri 10am–5pm, Sat 10am–1pm, 2–5pm; free) contains local artefacts, paintings, and collections on military history and railways.

The **Palace Demesne** covers 70 acres (28 hectares) of beautiful parkland, where the palace building and stables, designed in 1768, take centre stage. Today, it is a public park that hosts many events throughout the year. If you're feeling peckish then stop for a snack or something more filling at the **Moody Boar** (tel: 028-3752 9678; www.themoodyboar.com) a restored restaurant in the 18th-century palace stables.

Discovering planets

Armagh's Planetarium (College Hill; tel: 028-3752 3689; www.armaghplanet.com; Mon–Sat 10am–5pm) is popular with older children as well as adults. Astronomical shows, which must be pre-booked, have been enhanced by a major refurbishment to the Digital Theatre, including the world's most advanced digital projection system. There are also interactive exhibitions and an outdoor Astropark with scale models of the planets. There is free access to the grounds of the Observatory, of which the Planetarium is a part.

This way to the cathedrals.

Mourne Mountains shrouded in mist.

MOURNE MOUNTAINS

On the A28 southeast of Armagh is Markethill, where nearby **Gosford Forest Park** ❹ (tel: 028-3755 1277; closes at dusk; free) features a turreted mock-Norman castle. Continue on the A28 to Newry, the gateway to the Mountains of Mourne. Equidistant between Dublin and Belfast, the city of **Newry** ❺ was bound to prosper once the peace process began and the motorway was extended north and south.

The Newry and Mourne Museum and the tourist information centre are both in the restored 16th-century **Bagenal's Castle** (Castle Street; 028-3031 3182; www.bagenalscastle.com; Mon–Sat 10am–4.30pm, Sun 1.30–5pm; free).

Five miles (8km) southeast of Newry along the dual carriageway is the pretty seaside resort of **Warrenpoint**, celebrated for 'Blues in the Bay' each May, one of the finest blues festivals in the UK. A few minutes around the coast, **Rostrevor** ❻, sheltered by high hills, is smaller but prettier with a Victorian atmosphere.

A steep half-mile (0.8km) walk up the slopes of **Slievemartin** (1,595ft/486m) brings you to Cloghmore, a 'Big Stone' supposedly hurled by an Irish giant at a rival Scot. The geological explanation is more mundane, having to do with glacial drift.

Skirting round the Mourne Mountains, passing 14th-century Greencastle, takes you to the active fishing village of **Kilkeel** ❼, capital of the so-called 'Kingdom of Mourne'. Its idyllic location between mountain and sea makes it an ideal base from which to explore the mountains.

Moody Mournes

The Mournes are 'young' mountains (like the Alps) and their chameleon qualities attract walkers. One moment the granite is grey, the next pink. You walk by an isolated farmhouse, and within moments are in the middle of a wilderness. One minute, the Mournes justify all the songs written about them; the next, they become plain scrubland and unexceptional hills. The weather has a lot to do with this variety.

Brontës and Banbridge

The B27, running north from Kilkeel, takes us through the heart of the mountains.

Off the B27, the remote **Silent Valley Mountain Park** cradles a large dam, which supplies Belfast and County Down with water. This beautiful, tranquil spot is ideal for picnics and has an information centre.

Turn north at Hilltown onto the B25, and take the B7 at Rathfriland to Ballroney for the **Brontë Homeland Interpretive Centre** ❽ (Church Hill Road, Rathfriland; tel: 028-4062 3322; Mar–Sept Fri–Sun noon–4.30pm), a trail invented to capitalise on the fact that Patrick Brontë, father of Charlotte, Emily and Anne, was born nearby.

Join the A50 at Moneyslane and continue to **Banbridge** ❾, with its polar bear memorial to Captain Crozier, discoverer of the Northwest Passage. Just outside Banbridge on the A1 is the huge Bridgewater Park shopping centre.

Heading in the direction of Belfast, our tour finishes just off the A1 at **Hillsborough** ❿, packed with antique shops and English-style pubs, and rich in Georgian architecture.

Eating Out

Armagh

4 Vicars

4 Vicars Hill; tel: 028-3752 7772; www.4vicars.com; lunch Wed–Sun 10am–3pm, dinner Sat–Sun 6–8.30pm.

Three intimate dining rooms in a Georgian house beside the cathedral, 4 Vicars takes pride in local ingredients, such as Kilkeel cod, Loughgall baby vegetables and Richhill free-range chicken. Being in orchard country gives you the perfect excuse to plump for the Bramley Apple Pudding. ££

Banbridge

Blend & Batch

104 Newry Street; tel: 028-4023 8050; www.blendxbatch.com; daily 8am–8pm.

A blend of the best roasted coffee in town with home-style batch cooking in a sleek contemporary setting. From breakfast to lunch and on to afternoon cakes, you can't go far wrong. £

Hillsborough

The Parson's Nose

48 Lisburn Street; tel: 028-9262 3009; www.ballooinns.com; daily noon–9pm, Fri–Sat until 10pm.

This magical pub/restaurant conjures up the perfect old-world inn: roaring fires, stags' heads and low-vaulted ceilings. The most desirable food is inspired by local traditions and supports local artisan suppliers. ££

Warrenpoint

Fusion Restaurant

4 Duke Street; tel: 028-4175 3047; http://fusionwarrenpoint.co.uk; Mon–Thu 5–9pm, Fri–Sat noon–10pm, Sun noon–8.30pm.

Fusion delivers local ingredients with a Mediterranean twist in an urban vintage setting. There's a convivial atmosphere and an excellent cocktail list. Wild Irish venison with pear and plum compote, grilled red snapper in a Thai soy dressing and Mourne beer-battered Irish cod are amongst the choices. ££

Restaurant 23

The Balmoral Hotel, 13 Seaview; tel: 028-4175 3222; www.restaurant23.com; daily noon–2.30pm and 5.30–9.30pm.

A great team is in charge of this breezily relaxed first-floor waterfront restaurant located in the Balmoral Hotel. The enticing set menu and à la carte choices include milk-fed lamb from the Mourne Mountains, or pig 'n' fig – pork fillet wrapped in bacon, and washed down with a bottle of the locally brewed McArdle's Mourne stout. £££

Train carriages at the Ulster Folk and Transport Museum.

Tour 13

Around the Ards Peninsula

Covering around 115 miles (185km), this one-day tour explores every aspect of this area of outstanding scenic beauty with its rich heritage, history and culture.

The Ards Peninsula, 23 miles (37km) long, provides an excellent focus for a tour. North is the Gold Coast, with seaside resorts and excellent beaches, south is Portaferry where the journey continues via a ferry to attractive towns such as Downpatrick and Newcastle. To the west the road traverses the coast dotted with little fishing ports while east it follows both sides of Strangford Lough to discover a host of wildlife habitats.

Highlights

- Ulster Folk and Transport Museum
- Gold Coast beaches
- Mount Stewart
- Exploris
- Strangford Lough
- Newcastle

THE GOLD COAST

The A2 from Belfast city centre to Bangor runs through what locals describe as the 'Gold Coast'. **George Best Belfast City Airport** on this road is just a few minutes' drive from the heart of the city. Just past the airport, the attractive, residential town of **Holywood** ❶ has some good restaurants, cafés and craft shops. Only a 15-minute drive from the city centre, along Belfast Lough, it already begins to feel like the countryside. This is stockbroker country, where lush lawns meet mature woodland. Hillside sites, overlooking the shipping lanes, have traditionally lured the well-heeled. **Cultra**, 10 km (6 miles) this side of Bangor, has leafy lanes, splendid houses, and the resplendent Culloden Hotel. Yachting, golf and horse riding are popular pastimes here.

At Cultra Manor is the **Ulster Folk and Transport Museum ❷** (tel: 028-9042 8428; http://nmni.com/uftm; Mar–Sept Tue–Sun 10am–5pm, Oct–Feb until 4pm), one of Ireland's most popular tourist attractions. Farmhouses, cottages, churches and mills have been painstakingly reconstructed – often brick by brick.

Before reaching Bangor, a sign-posted detour on the B20 takes in the beaches of Helen's Bay, the nearby wooded **Crawfordsburn Country Park** (tel: 028-9185 3621; free), and the pretty village of Crawfordsburn with its lovely Old Inn.

Bangor

Bangor ❸, originally a small seaside resort, is noted for its abbey. The expensively rejuvenated seafront still has to gentrify some of its fast-food bars and souvenir shops to do justice to the spanking-new marina full of yachts and cruisers. Rowing around the bay in hired punts, and fishing trips from the pier, are evergreen attractions. **The North Down Museum** (Castle Park Avenue; tel: 028-9127 1200; www.northdownmuseum.com; Tue–Sat 10am–4.30pm, Sun noon–4.30pm, July & Aug also open Mondays; free) showcases 2,500-year-old swords, a 9th-century handbell and 400-year-old maps. The old Bangor has been overgrown by acres of new housing developments and shopping centres. It is a busy town with a weekly open-air market, plenty of pubs, restaurants and parks. The best beach is nearby Ballyholme Bay.

South of Bangor on the A21 towards Newtownards is **The Somme Heritage Centre** (233 Bangor

Exhibit, the Folk and Transport Museum.

Bangor Marina has berths for over 600 crafts.

Road; tel: 028-9182 3202; Apr–June and Sept Mon–Thu 10am–4pm, Sat 11am–4pm, July–Aug Mon–Sat 10am–5pm, Oct–Mar Mon–Thu 10am–4pm), with a reconstructed front-line trench from the World War I battle, on the first day of which more than 2,000 Ulster volunteer soldiers died.

Newtownards

Sprawling **Newtownards** ❹, at the head of **Strangford Lough**, is an old market town, dating from the 17th century. Today it's a bustling shopping centre with a blend of traditional shops, a fine sandstone town hall and a covered shopping centre. Overlooking the town is Scrabo Tower (Scrabo Country Park; tel: 028-9181 1491; http://scrabotower.com), a 19th-century memorial to the third marquess of Londonderry, offering splendid vistas of the lough and the soft-hilled countryside. The 2014 film *Dracula Untold* was shot here.

Coastal detour

The A2, southeast from Bangor, follows the coastal side of the peninsula. Between June and August, it's worth taking the detour to the pretty seaside village of **Groomsport** to see the two old fishermen's Cockle Row cottages, furnished c.1910. **Donaghadee** is notable for its colourful harbour and lighthouse, and summer boat trips. The twisting road passes quieter beaches at Ballywalter and Ballyhalbert, and the fishing port of **Portavogie**, which has occasional evening quayside fish auctions.

STRANGFORD LOUGH

Take the A20 along the east shore of the lough to **Mount Stewart** ❺ (tel: 028-4278 8387; www.nationaltrust.org.uk; gardens: daily 11am–6pm, house: by guided tour Apr–Oct daily 10am–5pm, Nov–Feb Sat–Sun only 10am–4pm), an 18th-century house with several fine gardens and a mild microclimate that fosters delicate plants untypical of the area. The gardens contain a variety of statues of griffins, satyrs and heraldic lions. The Temple of the Winds, an 18th-century octagonal folly in the grounds, offers a splendid view of the lough. Within the grounds of Mount Stewart take the time to follow the looped walking trails to appreciate the scale of the lough and its wildlife. 'Muck in at Mount Stewart' is one of several initiatives that empower children to learn more about nature through helping with conservation work on the estate.

East shore

South on the A20, the pretty village of **Greyabbey** has one of the most complete Cistercian abbeys in Ireland (tel: 028-9181 1491; Apr–Sept daily 10am–5pm, Oct–Mar Sun noon–4pm; free). Don't miss the medieval herb garden.

Travel to the tip of the peninsula to **Portaferry**, where you'll find **Exploris** ❻ (Castle Street; tel: 028-4272 8062; www.exploris.com; Apr–Oct daily 10am–6pm, Nov–Mar Mon–Sat 10am–5pm), Northern Ireland's only sea aquarium and seal sanctuary. Here you need to take the regular car ferry from the town, which chugs a slanted course to **Strangford** ❼. Near Strangford is the 18th-century Georgian mansion **Castle Ward** (tel: 028-4488 1204; www.nationaltrust.org.uk; house: mid-Mar–Oct daily noon–5pm, grounds: daily Apr–Sept 10am–8pm, Oct–Mar 10am–4pm), once the home of the lord of Bangor and now a National Trust property. Castle Ward was also used as a filming location for HBO's *Game of Thrones*. There are wildfowl in the 700-acre (280-hectare) grounds.

FOLLOW THE COAST

Take the A2 south from Strangford, which follows the coast passing through **Ardglass** ❽, where several ruined castles hint at its strategic importance in the Middle Ages. A stopover at Cloghy Rocks is a great place for viewing seals when the tide is right. At Clough continue on the A2 as the road almost comes back on itself heading towards Newcastle. This stretch passes Dundrum Castle, Ireland's finest Anglo-Norman castle. **Dundrum** village is a source of wonderful local seafood with an excellent pub restaurant in which to enjoy it (see page 113).

The Victorian resort of **Newcastle** ❾, where the **Mountains of Mourne** do, as the Percy French ballad describes, 'run down to the sea', is famous for the **Royal County Down links**, rated in the world's top 20 golf courses. The town, which has a fine sandy beach, is small and picturesque with the 2,796ft (850m) peaks of Slieve Donard forming a perfect backdrop.

Strangford Lough

The lough, one of Europe's most important wildlife sites, has more than 2,000 species of marine animal. Its wetlands support 25,000 wildfowl and 50,000 waders. Several species of tern arrive in summer, and in winter the lough is thought to support 75 percent of the world's Brent geese. Ireland's largest colony of common seals breed here and 30ft (9m) basking sharks are sometimes seen in the lough's entrance.

Birdlife on Strangford Lough.

The sea inlet of Strangford Lough.

DOWNPATRICK

Take the A50 5 miles (8km) inland from Newcastle to Castlewellan, then continue east on the A25 to **Downpatrick** ⑩. The name is a marriage of Patrick, this island's patron saint, and the Irish for fort *(dún)*. You can follow Patrick's story in a superb exhibition at the **St Patrick Centre** (Lower Market Street; tel: 028-4461 9000; www.saintpatrickcentre.com; year round Mon–Sat 9am–5pm, July–Aug also Sun 1–5pm). Many people picnic near here by the healing waters of the bathhouses at Struell's St Patrick's Wells. Also in Downpatrick is the excellent **Down County Museum** (tel: 028-4461 5218; www.downcountymuseum.com; Mon–Fri 10am–5pm, Sun 1–5pm; free), housed in a 1798 jailhouse.

WEST SHORE

From Downpatrick take the A22 back along the scenic west shore of Strangford Lough, a conservation area, noted for myriad islands, most of which are sunken drumlins, the smooth glacial hillocks that characterise the landscape.

Mahee Island, accessible by bridge, has the remains of Nendrum Abbey (tel: 028-9181 1491; daily Apr–Sept 10am–5pm, Oct–Mar noon–4pm; free), destroyed by Vikings in

Steam travel.

Steam railway

A hundred yards or so away from the St Patrick Centre is the atmospheric **Downpatrick and County Down Steam Railway** (tel: 028-4461 5779; www.downrail.org), which excites children as much as it does steam enthusiasts. It runs at weekends from June to September, as well as a special Lapland Express at Christmas.

AD974. Castle Espie Wetlands Centre (78 Ballydrain Road; tel: 028-9187 4146) is the base for Ireland's largest collection of ducks, geese and swans.

Comber ⑪, 9 miles (14km) southeast of Belfast at the head of Strangford Lough, was a linen town and still has a working mill. The town centre retains its old character with single-storey cottage shops. From Comber, the A22 merges onto the A20 and leads back to the city centre.

Fishing at Donaghadee.

Eating Out

Bangor

The Boathouse

1A Seacliff Road; tel: 028-9146 9253; http://boathousebangor.com; Wed–Sat 5.30–9.30pm, Sat also 12.30–2.30pm, Sun 1–8pm.
Located in the old Harbour Masters Office beside the marina. Original features have been retained to provide an enchanting setting in which to savour superior locally sourced food. £££

Comber

Old Post Office

191 Killinchy Road, Lisbane; tel: 028-9754 3335; www.oldpostofficelisbane.co.uk; Mon–Sat 9am–5pm.
On the shore of Strangford Lough, these quaint tearooms have delicious home-made cakes and wholesome lunches. £

Donaghadee

Grace Neill's Bar & Grill

33 High Street; tel: 028-9188 9631; www.graceneills.com; Mon–Wed, Sun noon–11pm, Thu until midnight, Fri–Sat until 1am.
Established in 1611, this historic pub offers lashings of character and atmosphere, serving good-value traditional dishes with an imaginative spin. ££

Dundrum

Bucks Head Inn

77 Main Street; tel: 028-4375 1868; Mon–Sat noon–9pm, Sun until 8.30pm, closed Mon Oct–Apr.
Renowned for a warm welcome, this cosy bar has an open fire, while the modern restaurant makes the most of seasonal produce, especially the Dundrum oysters and mussels. ££

Holywood

Fontana

61a High Street; tel: 028-9080 9988; www.restaurantfontana.com; lunch Tue–Fri noon–2.30pm, Sun noon–4pm, dinner Tue–Sat 5.30–9pm.
Winner of a Michelin Bib Gourmand award in 2017. This is a real neighbourhood favourite that has stood the test of time. Try the pan-roasted monkfish with miso or the Portavogie prawn risotto. £££

Newcastle

Hugh McCanns

119–21 Central Promenade; tel: 028-4372 2487; www.hughmccanns.com; daily 10am–9.30pm.
Nestled in a great location with stunning mountain and sea views. The family-owned café-bar-cum-deli is ideal for a light lunch or something more substantial. It is renowned for its steaks and mouth-watering desserts. ££

The Odyssey at Queen's Quay.

W5

Popular race meetings are held at Down Royal Racecourse.

Travel Tips

Active Pursuits

The north of Ireland has such diverse terrain it would be hard to match the quality and range of active pursuits. Loughs, rivers and coastal waters offer second-to-none water sports and fishing, while mountains and cliffs provide an adventure playground for climbers and walkers. Multi-activity centres across the counties have a host of challenging pursuits such as canoeing, abseiling, kayaking, rock climbing, archery and lots more.

Greater Belfast (on which the following listings focus) is crammed with indoor activities to entertain the family when the weather is not so good. One of the city's most appealing attributes is its openness and space, ideal for walking, cycling (see page 121) and golf. There's no excuse not to get active, but if you prefer to watch rather than take part, there is usually a match or sporting event going on somewhere.

BOWLING

Odyssey Bowl, Odyssey Pavilion, 2 Queen's Quay; tel: 028-9045 2100; www.odysseybowl.co.uk. This 20-lane bowling alley also has a pool bar, arcade and diner, and is fully licenced. **Xtreme Bowling**, Dundonald International Ice Bowl, 111 Old Dundonald Road; tel: 028-9080 9100; www.theicebowl.com. Twenty minutes from the city centre is Northern Ireland's only public Olympic-size ice rink, which also houses a bowling alley and children's indoor adventure centre.

GOLF

Northern Ireland is truly a golfer's paradise and Belfast has 11 courses within the city boundary, plus scores of others throughout Northern Ireland. **Balmoral Golf Club**, 518 Lisburn Road; tel: 028-9038 1514; www.balmoralgolf.com, is literally minutes from the city centre, nearly as venerable as Royal Belfast and more easily accessible. A 2,276yd/m parkland course, it was here that champion Irish golfer Fred Daly learnt the ropes. Good clubhouse, too. **Belvoir Park**, 73 Church Road, Newtownbreda; tel: 028-9049 1693; www.belvoirparkgolfclub.com, has hosted Irish opens and was judged by Gary Player to be one of the world's best parkland courses. It's also one of the most beautiful. **Citigolf Belfast**, Regus House, Cromac Street; tel: 028-9023 2232; www.citigolfbelfast.com, is an indoor golf simulator that allows golfers to play on 57 of the top golf courses in the world, without having to leave the Belfast. **Royal Belfast**, Station Road, Craigavad, Holywood; tel: 028-9042 8165; www.royalbelfast.com. The best of them all, and the oldest club in Ireland. Not always the easiest to visit (though staying at the adjacent Culloden Hotel earns you special access), it has magnificent views of Belfast Lough and a challenging course that attracts leading golfers.

SWIMMING

Lagan Valley Lisburn LeisurePlex, 18 Leisure Park, Lisburn; tel: 028-9267 2121; www.lisburnleisurepark.co.uk. For the longest, fastest and wettest water rides, as well as a 25yd/m pool, a diving pool, an aquatic play area for younger children, a gym and a spa.

WALKING

Belfast has miles of designated walkways by the river, across hills or through nature reserves and parks. Besides the walking tours available (see page 119), there are various groups and organisations to help you gain the best walking experience.

Active kids

Kids – especially aspiring farmers – adore Streamvale Open Farm (38 Ballyhanwood Road; tel: 028-9048 3244; www.streamvale.com; Apr–Oct Mon–Sat 10.30am–5pm, Sun 2–5pm) with animals to feed, nature trails, play areas, and pony, quad and tractor rides. You can watch the cows being milked every afternoon.

Pickie Funpark (Marine Gardens, Bangor; tel. 028-9145 0746; http://pickiefunpark.com; summer daily 9am–9pm, winter Sat–Sun 9am–4pm) was given a £2.6-million facelift in 2012. Giant pedal swans, a steam train, children's electric-powered cars, a mini golf course, splash pads and playgrounds are the main attractions here.

Streamvale Farm resident.

Northern Walking Partnership, tel: 0770 799 4600; www.northernwalking.com. Passionate about hill walking, this group organises walks of varying lengths and types in and around Belfast and beyond, led by qualified guides.

SPECTATOR SPORTS

Athletics

Mary Peter's Track, Old Coach Road; tel: 028-9060 2707; www.athleticsni.org. International athletics meetings are held at this track, named after the Northern Irish Olympic gold medallist. **Belfast City Marathon**, tel: 028-9060 5922; www.belfastcitymarathon.com. The marathon takes place on the first Monday in May; a 26-mile (39km) trot around the city.

Ball games

Ulster Rugby, The Kingspan Stadium, 134 Mount Merrion Avenue; tel: 028-9049 3222; www.ulsterrugby.com. The Ulster rugby union team play both national and international fixtures at their Kingspan headquarters. **Windsor Park**, Windsor Avenue; tel: 028-9024 4198; www.irishfa.com, is home to the Northern Ireland football team. Northern Ireland qualified for their first European Championships in 2016, where they advanced to the second round. **Casement Park**, Andersonstown Road; tel: 028-3752 1900; www.casementpark.ie is the place to enjoy Gaelic games, the national sports of Ireland.

Gaelic football.

Hurling has Gaelic origins and a team comprises 15 players.

Horse racing

Down Royal Racecourse, Maze, Lisburn; tel: 028-9262 1256; www.downroyal.com. This historic racecourse, 10 miles (16km) south of the city centre, has a series of popular meetings throughout the year.

Ice hockey

LBM Belfast Giants, Odyssey Arena, 2 Queen's Quay; tel: 028-9046 0044; www.belfastgiants.com. The Giants have built up a huge fan base for this exhilarating sport. The 28 home games per season (Sept–Apr) are attended by a capacity crowd of more than 4,000.

Themed Holidays

A holiday in Northern Ireland can be more than just the normal sightseeing trip. The region's diversity lends itself to all sorts of interesting ways to spend a vacation.

CREATIVE BREAKS

Belfast Cookery School, 53–4 Castle Street; tel: 028-9023 4722; www.belfastcookeryschool.com. The team behind the Mourne Seafood bar run culinary classes for all abilities.

Ballydougan Pottery, Gilford, Co. Armagh; tel: 028-3834 2201; www.ballydouganpottery.co.uk. Pottery workshops, ranging from hour-long courses to creative weekends, are held at this innovative craft studio.

HEALTHY OPTIONS

Galgorm Resort & Spa, Galgorm, Co. Antrim; tel: 028-2588 1001; www.galgorm.com. Just 30 minutes from Belfast, Galgorm provides ultimate luxury with its unique thermal village, hammam, Celtic sauna and group treatment suites.

Lake Isle Retreat, Derrylin, Co. Fermanagh; www.lakeisleretreats.com. Spiritual retreats with an emphasis on mindfulness, yoga and vegetarian cooking on Hare Krishna island on idyllic Lough Erne.

Time for contemplation in relaxing surroundings.

HORSE RIDING

Sheans Horse Farm, 38 Cooleeran Road, Armoy, Ballymoney, Co. Antrim; tel: 07759 320 434; www.sheanshorsefarm.com. Tuition and off-road hacking holidays in the North Antrim hills, an area of outstanding natural beauty.

WALKING

A Way a Wee Walk, 161a Andersonstown Road, Belfast; tel: 078-3770 3643; www.awayaweewalk.com. Daily walking tours of the Giant's Causeway cliff path, as well as hiking holidays around the Glens of Antrim and the Mountains of Mourne, staying in authentic B&B accommodation.

THEMED WALKS

Ghost Walk (tel: 079 0435 0339; www.ghostwalkbelfast.com; Wed and Fri at 9.30pm) explores the depths of Titanic's Dock and Pumphouse for 90 minutes of spine-tingling ghost hunting.

Game of Thrones Tour (tel: 028-9024 7797; www.gameofthronestours.tv; Mon 5pm) visits actual filming locations of the award-winning series. Guides are hugely enthusiastic.

Titanic Walk & Tram Tours (tel: 079-0435 0339; www.titanicwalk.com) take you around the shipyard where Titanic was built.

Belfast Food Tour (http://tasteandtour.co.uk) takes you 'off the 'eaten track', starting in St George's Market and finishing in the Cathedral Quarter. Lead by award-winning foodie Caroline Wilson.

Belfastology Walking Tour (tel: 075-2309 575; www.belfastology.com; Mon–Fri 4pm, 6pm, 8pm, Sat–Sun every 2 hours from 8am–10pm). An eclectic walking tour of the city's history, architecture and people. Departs from City Hall.

Practical Information

GETTING THERE

By air

Belfast International (tel: 028-9448 4848; www.belfastairport.com), 19 miles (30 km) northwest of the city, is Northern Ireland's busiest airport with connections to the rest of the UK, Europe and the US. Numerous daily services link Belfast International with Heathrow, Stansted and many other UK airports.

George Best Belfast City Airport, (tel: 028-9093 9093; www.belfastcityairport.com) 3 miles (5km) east of the city centre, has flights to several European cities and UK provincial airports, plus London's City, Heathrow, Gatwick, Luton and Stansted.

The Airport Express 300 bus (tel: 028-9066 6630; Mon–Fri, every 15 minutes peak times, less frequent Sat–Sun) runs to the city centre from the International Airport. George Best Airport has rail links to Great Victoria Street and a direct bus link to the city centre every 40 minutes. Taxis are plentiful from both airports.

Taxi ranks are dotted around the city.

By sea

Stena Line (tel: 028-9077 9090; www.stenaline.co.uk) has up to six sailings a day between Belfast and Cairnryan in Scotland. P&O Irish Sea (tel: 0871 664 4777; www.poferries.com) sails between Cairnryan and Larne, just northeast of Belfast.

GETTING AROUND

By bus

Translink (tel: 028-9066 6630; www.translink.co.uk) operates the bus network. The Metro bus serves Belfast and the suburbs; services usually start and end around City Hall. Fares can be paid on board or you can buy Smartlink multi-journey tickets (travel cards are available in outlets displaying the Metro Smartlink sign, or you can purchase via the mLink app). Goldline Express and other Ulsterbus services to the rest of Northern Ireland and beyond operate from the Europa or Laganside Bus Centres.

By train

Northern Ireland Railways, also operated by Translink, run services east to Bangor, northeast to Larne, northwest to Derry and south to Dublin. Commuter trains from Central or Great Victoria Street stations to the Botanic Station provide easy access to the campus area.

By taxi

There are taxi ranks at City Hall, the Crown Bar, airports and main stations. Drivers at Castle Junction pack London-style taxis until full for a particular direction; they also organise tailored tours. Alternatively, call a 'radio cab' such as Value Cabs (tel: 028-9080 9080; www.valuecabs.co.uk) or

The Metro bus in the city centre.

fonaCAB (tel: 028-9033 3333; www.fonacab.com). Public taxis can be hailed when they have a 'for hire' sign illuminated. Fares are set by the Department of the Environment; private firms have their own rates. If they do not display a meter, ask for the approximate cost in advance.

By car

The city has many car parks and lots of on-street pay-and-display parking. Donegall Place and its tributaries are pedestrianised, but only in theory. Drive on the left; speed limits, with clearly signed exceptions, are 30mph (50km/h) in built-up areas, 60mph (95km/h) outside built-up areas and 70mph (112km/h) on motorways. Most recognised car hire firms operate from the airports and have city offices. Options include Argus Car Hire (tel: 020 3740 9859; www.arguscarhire.com); Avis Rent a Car (tel: 028-9032 9258; www.avis.co.uk); and Enterprise Rent a Car (tel: 028-9066 6767; www.enterprise.com).

By bike

Completion of the Millennium National Cycling Network added lots more opportunities for cycling in and around the city, with dedicated paths along the River Lagan (see page 71), mandatory cycle lanes in the centre, and out-of-town tracks (free maps from Belfast Welcome Centre). One of the newest, opened in 2013, is the tranquil Comber Greenway which runs eight miles along a disused railway line from East Belfast to Comber. The route, also suitable for walkers, starts at the

Going green

Belfast is becoming increasingly bicycle friendly. 'Cycle to Work' is a government initiative to encourage local people to leave their cars at home. It is part of the city's Green Transport Plan and includes helping employees buy bicycles tax free. The Belfast Bike scheme (www.belfastbikes.co.uk) is a public bike-hire initiative that has the same aim – it now has 40 docking stations dotted across the city.

Outside the city, the Ulster Way now stretches a staggering 625 miles (1,000km) around Northern Ireland, making it the longest circular walking path in the United Kingdom and Ireland. Pick up the Belfast by Bike leaflet at the Welcome Centre or visit www.drdni.gov.uk/roads/cycling for tips, detailed information and a map with the city's main cycling routes.

Big Fish sculpture beside the Queen Elizabeth II Bridge, follows the riverside past the Odyssey Arena, takes in the *Titanic* attractions, the C. S. Lewis statue and Parliament Buildings at Stormont. The best way to hire a bike is to sign up to the public Belfast bike-hire scheme (www.belfastbikes.co.uk).

FACTS FOR THE VISITOR

Travellers with disabilities

The official tourist information service for Belfast and Northern Ireland (www.visitbelfast.com) has teamed up with Disabled Go (www.disabledgo.com) to assist people with disabilities. It is dedicated to improving access and provides a national access guide on the internet; a total of 986 venues have been researched, including visitor attractions, shops, restaurants, bars and services.

Most buses, trains and taxis have wheelchair access. Disability Action (tel: 028-9029 7880); www.disabilty action.org) has useful information, too.

EMERGENCIES

Ambulance, fire, police: dial 999.

For medical and dental emergencies, the main Accident and Emergency hospital is Belfast City Hospital (51 Lisburn Road; tel: 028-9032 9241).

OPENING HOURS

City-centre shops are generally open Mon–Sat 9.30am–5.30pm (Thu until 9pm). Some larger stores open Sun 1–5pm. Neighbourhood stores and garage forecourt convenience shops often open much longer – 24 hours in many cases.

TOURIST INFORMATION

Major towns throughout the north of Ireland have a tourist information office.

The Belfast Welcome Centre (8–10 Donegall Square North; tel: 028-9024 6609; www.visitbelfast.com) is a one-stop tourist centre with information on accommodation, visitor attractions, tours, events and transport, both for Belfast, the rest of Northern Ireland and the Irish Republic. Multilingual staff can book accommodation, concerts and tours. They have a shop, left-luggage facility, bureau de change and internet facilities, as well as drinks machines. They also have information centres at the city's two airports.

The local tourist office in Derry

The Ulster Orchestra performing at the Waterfront Hall.

(44 Foyle Street; tel: 028-7126 7284; www.derryvisitor.com) can supply information on the city, book accommodation and give advice on the surrounding area.

ENTERTAINMENT

Belfast has earned a surprisingly good reputation for a new generation of stylish bars and nightclubs, and hotel bars are particularly polished. Traditional pubs (see page 38) remain popular and often provide a venue for live music. There is plenty of opportunity, too, for a night at the theatre or cinema, plus comedy events and concerts.

Nightlife

The streets around City Hall and Donegall Square are rich with a number of trendy bars: a big draw is Chinawhite (43 Franklin Street; tel. 028-9024 8000; http://chinawhitebelfast.com). This high-end nightclub is a sister club to the London original and has stunning Asian-inspired decor. At No. 42, The Perch (tel. 028-9024 8000; www.theperchbelfast.com) attracts a hip crowd to its cool modern rooftop bar. Rita's Beer & Cocktail Club (44 Franklin Street, tel: 028-9024 8000) is a unique spot with retro interiors and a large and inventive range of cocktails.

In Queen's Quarter, the Alibi (23–31 Bradbury Place; tel: 028-9023 3131; http://alibibelfast.com), situated in the heart of the nightlife district, is lively yet sophisticated, with a great music mix.

Theatre/cinema/music

The main music, theatre and comedy venues are the Ulster Hall (see page 17), Waterfront Hall (see page 59), Grand Opera House (see page 24), Belfast Empire (42 Botanic Avenue; tel: 028-9024 9276; www.thebelfastempire.com) and SSE Arena (see page 86). For cinema, the Odeon Belfast (1 Victoria Square; tel: 028-9033 3424) has eight screens. Other complexes can be found at the Movie House cinemas (www.moviehouse.co.uk) in York Street and the Dublin Road, and the Odyssey cinemas at The Odyssey pavilion (see page 85). Non-mainstream films can be seen at the Queen's Film Theatre (see page 51).

Live music in a pub.

Gay and lesbian

Centred around the Cathedral Quarter, The Kremlin (96 Donegall Street; tel: 028-9031 6060), a Soviet-themed nightclub, forms the hub of Belfast's increasingly visible gay and lesbian scene. Another stylish option is Union Street (www.unionstreetbar.com), housed in a converted Victorian shoe factory at 8–14 Union Street right in the city centre.

The Belfast Pride Festival (www.belfastpride.com) celebrates with a new confidence, hosting a week of parties, concerts, talks, discos, and a parade around the city centre, in late July or early August. A useful contact is the Northern Ireland Gay Rights Association (tel: 028-9066 4111; http://nigra.org.uk).

The Belfast LGBT centre is located in the Cathedral Quarter at Nos 23–31 Warring Street (tel. 028-9031 9030; http://lgbtni.org).

Accommodation

Belfast is a popular business destination midweek, so weekend rates tend to be cheaper and you may be able to negotiate a better rate with some hotels. Many offer good deals online or at the last minute. B&Bs and guesthouses are also good value, offering easy-going Irish hospitality and some excellent breakfasts.

Prices for a standard double room for one night with breakfast
£ = under £80
££ = £80–£150
£££ = over £150

BELFAST

Arnie's Backpackers
63 Fitzwilliam Street; tel: 028-9024 2867; www.arniesbackpackers.co.uk.
A 27-bed Queen's Quarter hostel based in an old Victorian town house, Arnie's creates a comfortable atmosphere with its friendly welcome. With prices starting at only £16 a night, this is a real find. £

The Piano Lounge in Hastings Europa Hotel.

Benedicts Hotel
7–21 Bradbury Place; tel: 028-9059 1999; www.benedictshotel.co.uk.
Four-star boutique-style hotel with 32 individually styled rooms featuring feather-topped mattresses and goose-down duvets. It is known for its excellent restaurant, which uses local produce, and its lively bar. ££

Bullitt
40a Church Lane; tel: 028-9590 0600; www.bullitthotel.com.
Named and styled after the uber-cool Steve McQueen film, this is Belfast's latest hip hotel. Breakfast is served in a paper bag and the rooftop ski-themed bar, Baltic, has great views over Victoria Square. The rooms are small but very comfortable and are stripped bare of 'over-the-top' extras to keep prices down. ££

Crescent Town House
13 Lower Crescent Road; tel: 028-9032 3349; www.crescenttownhouse.com.
This is Belfast's original boutique hotel in a stylishly restored 19th-century house in the Queen's Quarter. It's discreetly tucked away yet on the doorstep of this nightlife district. It has its own chic bar and popular brasserie, Metro Kitchen, next door. ££

Fitzwilliam Hotel
1–3 Great Victoria Street; tel: 028-9044 2080; www.fitzwilliamhotelbelfast.com.
The interior of this eco-friendly hotel is contemporary, sleek and elegantly designed, with environmentally friendly features built into the fabric of the building. £££

Hastings Europa Hotel
Great Victoria Street; tel: 028-9027 1066; www.hastingshotels.com.
Belfast's most famous hotel has been refurbished but retains its cachet from

troubled times in the past. It's in a good central location, opposite the famous Crown Liquor Saloon. ££–££

Madison's

59–63 Botanic Avenue; tel: 028-9050 9800; www.madisonshotel.com.

This small contemporary hotel is one of the best options in the Queen's Quarter. Bright rooms and a stylish café-restaurant serving locally sourced food are among the attractions. ££

Malmaison Belfast

34–8 Victoria Street; tel: 028-9022 0200; www.malmaison.com.

Near the city centre, this imaginative new conversion from two beautiful Victorian seed warehouses has dramatic decor plus a popular brasserie and Art Deco bar. £££

Luxury awaits you at the Merchant Hotel.

Merchant Hotel

35–9 Waring St; tel: 028-9023 4888; www.themerchanthotel.com.

This opulent five-star hotel in the heart of the Cathedral Quarter aims to be ranked alongside Claridge's in London. A £16-million expansion added 38 rooms and a rooftop garden. £££

The stylish bar at Malmaison Belfast.

The Old Rectory

148 Malone Road; tel: 028-9066 7882; www.anoldrectory.co.uk.

This delightful Victorian guesthouse in South Belfast is renowned for its fine breakfasts. The rooms are beautiful, with great attention to detail. ££

Ten Square

10 Donegall Square South; tel: 028-9024 1001; www.tensquare.co.uk.

A Victorian linen warehouse transformed into a luxury hotel. The accent on indulgence, such as goose-down pillows and Bang & Olufsen plasma screens, attracts a celebrity following. £££

Wellington Park Hotel

21 Malone Road; tel: 028-9038 1111; www.wellingtonparkhotel.com.

The Wellington, or 'Welly Park' as it's locally known, is a three-star, family-run establishment, close to Queen's University. One of Belfast's busiest hotels, it is especially good value for people with children as under 5s stay free of charge. £

NORTH

Bushmills Inn Hotel

9 Dunluce Road, Bushmills, County Antrim; tel: 028-2073 3000; www.bushmillsinn.com.

The Old Inn at Crawfordsburn, County Down.

Located in a coach house and stables and believed to date from 1608, this four-star hotel features turf fires, gaslights and luxurious rooms. £££

Maldron Hotel Derry
Butcher Street, Derry, County Londonderry; tel: 028-7137 1000; www.maldronhotelderry.com.
The only hotel within the old walls of the city; well placed for restaurants and bars. The bright, airy rooms have well-appointed bathrooms. £–££

WEST

Ard Na Breatha
Drumrooske Middle, Donegal, County Donegal; tel: 074-972 2288; www.ardnabreatha.com.
On the edge of Donegal town, tucked away in a residential area but backing onto farmland, this guesthouse has an ecotourism award. Lovely atmosphere, country-style rooms and scrumptious breakfasts. ££

Killyhevlin Hotel
Dublin Road, Enniskillen, County Fermanagh; tel: 028-6632 3481; www.killyhevlin.com.
Push the boat out and stay at this luxury hotel and spa with an idyllic lakeland setting. Seventy individually decorated rooms, good food and a health club, pool and gym. ££

EAST

The Old Inn
Main Street, Crawfordsburn, County Down; tel: 028-9185 3255; www.theoldinn.com.
An atmospheric inn 25 minutes' drive from Belfast centre. A favourite of C.S. Lewis, who grew up nearby. ££

Portaferry Hotel
10 The Strand, Portaferry, County Down; tel: 028-4272 8231; www.portaferryhotel.com.
Several of this attractive hotel's 14 rooms overlook Strangford Lough. It makes a good base for exploring both the lough and the local historic homes and gardens. ££

SOUTHEAST

Burrendale Hotel and Country Club
51 Castlewellan Road, Newcastle, County Down; tel: 028-4372 2599; www.burrendale.com.
Just outside the seaside resort of Newcastle and right on the edge of the Mountains of Mourne, this hotel is particularly popular with golfers playing the local courses and is renowned for its good food. ££

Index

Credits

Insight Guides Great Breaks Belfast
Editor: Helen Fanthorpe
Authors: Mary Conneely, Ian Hill, Seth Linder, Brian Bell, Jackie Staddon and Hilary Weston
Update Production: Apa Digital
Head of Production: Rebeka Davies
Picture Editor: Tom Smyth
Cartography Update: Carte
Photo credits: Alamy 19, 20T, 25, 44T, 60B, 112B; Fitzwilliam Hotel 21B; Getty Images 8/9, 12B, 14, 26B, 44B, 74, 91B; iStock 9, 91T, 111, 119; Kevin Cummins/Apa Publications 4/5, 6ML, 6MC, 6ML, 6MC, 7T, 7M, 7TR, 7MR, 7BR, 7M, 10T, 11, 12T, 13, 16T, 16B, 17, 18, 20B, 21T, 22, 23B, 23T, 24B, 24T, 26T, 28, 30TL, 30TC, 30MC, 31, 32, 33, 35, 36, 37, 38TL, 38ML, 39T, 43, 45, 46B, 48, 50, 51, 52T, 52B, 53, 55, 56T, 56B, 58T, 58B, 59B, 59T, 60T, 61, 62, 63T, 63B, 64T, 64B, 66, 68TL, 68ML, 72, 73, 75, 76, 78, 79, 80, 82TL, 82ML, 83T, 86, 88, 90, 92, 93B, 94, 95B, 95T, 96, 98, 99, 100, 101, 102, 103, 104, 105, 106, 108, 109, 110, 112, 113, 115, 117, 120, 121, 123, 125B, 126; Malmaison 65, 125T; Mary Evans Picture Library 10B; Northern Ireland Tourist Board 40, 41, 43, 46T, 69T, 70, 84, 93T, 118B, 118T, 122, 124; Presseye/INPHO/REX/Shutterstock 116
Cover credits: Shutterstock (all front cover)

CONTACT US:
Every effort has been made to provide accurate information in this publication, but changes are inevitable. The publisher cannot be responsible for any resulting loss, inconvenience or injury. We would appreciate it if readers would call our attention to any errors or outdated information. We also welcome your suggestions; please contact us at: hello@insightguides.com

Third Edition 2017

Printed in China by CTPS

Distribution
UK, Ireland and Europe: Apa Publications (UK) Ltd; sales@insightguides.com
United States and Canada: Ingram Publisher Services; ips@ingramcontent.com
Australia and New Zealand: Woodslane; info@woodslane.com.au
Southeast Asia: Apa Publications (SN) Pte; singaporeoffice@insightguides.com
Hong Kong, Taiwan and China: Apa Publications (HK) Ltd; hongkongoffice@insightguides.com
Worldwide: Apa Publications (UK) Ltd; sales@insightguides.com
Special Sales, Content Licensing and CoPublishing
Insight Guides can be purchased in bulk quantities at discounted prices. We can create special editions, personalised jackets and corporate imprints tailored to your needs. sales@insightguides.com; www.insightguides.biz